WOULD YOU
DO IT
FOR ME?

Responding to the Voice of God

Gael B. Hogan

RIVER BIRCH PRESS

Mesa, Arizona

ISBN 978-1-956365-78-8 (print)
ISBN 978-1-956365-79-5 (e-book)
For Worldwide Distribution
Printed in the U.S.A.

River Birch Press
P.O. Box 7341
Mesa, AZ 85216

ACKNOWLEDGMENTS

This book is in memory of my mom and dad who did all that they could for me—always. To my church family, brothers and sisters in Christ who have poured love and encouragement into me, thank you too. Sherry, Lynn, Tracy, Maureen, John, and Camrin—your particular acts of obedience made this possible.

To my dear friends who read this manuscript before anyone else, thank you for your honesty and integrity. I know it was hard to read the manuscript and act as eyes and ears for me, but you did exactly as I asked and made me better in the process. I can't thank you enough.

To my children: Brook, Adam, Peter, Alexander, Allegra, and Max. I am so proud of you. God has truly blessed me with your lives. This book is for you. To my other children: Keith, Jenn, and Nicki, and all my grandchildren. God has given me the increase, and I know I'm blessed.

To my spiritual children: watching you grow is one of the biggest joys in my life. I love how my garden grows.

And to my husband, Michael, thank you. I can't tell you how much I appreciate the love, freedom, and protection you have given me. Thank you for everything. I love you so much.

And to the many people whose names and stories are not mentioned in this book but are written between the lines, thank you from the bottom of my heart. What you did for us—planting and sowing into our lives—was for God alone.

But I want you to know, brethren, that the things
which happened to me have actually turned out
for the furtherance of the gospel
(Philippians 1:12 NKJV).

TABLE OF CONTENTS

PREFACE

In writing this book I wanted to open up a window, pull back the curtains, and let people peek into my life and my relationship with God, our Father. So many people want to know how to relate to God. If you know how to talk or express yourself, then you can have a relationship with Him. I subscribe to what the old hymn says that as I walk with Him and talk with Him, He will tell me I am His own I believe that is what Adam and Eve were created to do, and what Jesus died to restore. No pious religious prayers were required—just walking and talking to cultivate fellowship, relationship, and intimacy.

I want to open up my life to people who are asking how to have an intimate relationship with the Lord. They want to know how to pray. They want to know how much time to spend with the Lord. They want to know the physical and emotional process they might encounter in being obedient. Sometimes people even ask me if I ever feel like I'm going crazy. They also want to know about the mistakes I've made and what I've learned. In sharing some of the slices of my life, I want to answer these questions. I want to encourage people to know the joy of knowing God and following Him. But this relationship is not for me alone. This is what God intended for everyone.

This is why Jesus died on the cross. This is the good news. My hope and prayer is that this book will help you recognize, relate, and respond to the One who loves you.

And please know that what He has done for me, He will do for you too.

INTRODUCTION

Jesus was a wonderful storyteller. He was the best kind of storyteller because He kept His narratives short and to the point. He didn't have pictures to go along with the events He described, but He had illustrations. People came from all over to hear Him, and even the children sat at His feet.

Jesus used parables to make His points, to teach, and to answer questions. Oftentimes a simple statement could not convey the depth of meaning that a story could. Through His accounts, we see through His eyes and into His heart. And while people today have difficulty in memorizing a Scripture or even in remembering what to pick up at the store, they can remember a story.

The Lord still uses descriptions of life experiences to touch people's hearts and to reveal who He is. Stories are testimonies to the fact that He cares about us. He loves us. Throughout the writing of this book, I never lost sight of all the people who have their own adventures to chronicle with books inside of them—witnesses to the fact that Jesus is real. He is ALIVE! Throughout our lives, God proves His Word and His life are true. This book is a series of stories that chronicle the reality of Jesus in my own life. Over and over again He has proven Himself to me. He is faithful. He will never leave me or forsake me. His Word is true, and He loves me.

As I complete this book, I realize what a journey of faith and obedience it has been. I didn't want to write a book, but I couldn't deny what I knew in my heart that God had called me to do. I don't even know where this is going, but I know I've been faithful to obey. I have no expectations beyond finishing this project; it's all up to Him now. But I've struggled. Sitting down every day to work at this has been a challenge. Interruptions and distractions often tried to keep me from being focused. Instead of relieving me of the hindrances, God strengthened my resolve to persevere.

Not all of the obstacles have been physical. The biggest one has been a lack of confidence. I am reminded of a well-known actor that I interviewed backstage at a Broadway performance in which he was starring. He became sick in the bathroom because of nerves before every performance, yet he would go out and give the performance of his life night after night. So even though I've had some anxiety as I sought to follow God, like that actor I've given it my all every time I sat down to put my heart out on paper.

The Lord has been gracious to encourage me daily. He told me once to look at myself as a storyteller. Somehow that made the task easier to digest. In my mind, being a storyteller wasn't as daunting as being a "writer." I remember when the Lord said to me, "Just do it," and I finally wrote the first chapter. I was so excited as the words started to come and the stories poured out of me.

When I was concerned that anyone could do what I was doing and write what I was writing, He said, "You aren't writing anything new; you are just writing it in a new way." How freeing that was; and it's what Scripture says. Ecclesiastes 1:9 (AMP) reads, "There is nothing new under the sun."

I share this with you because some of you who are reading this are being convicted by the Holy Spirit to step out. Just like Moses and Jeremiah (and me, I might add), you have given all your reasons why you can't do something or be used by God. God has been calling you to do something for Him. He wants to use you as a vessel. He wants to express Himself through your personality, your gifts, and your life experiences to touch others. Trying is more important to Him—and even making some mistakes—than doing nothing at all. This book is about that. It's about lifestyle and process; it's about responding to God. Each time one of us is obedient to Him, the kingdom is furthered just a little bit more. So just do it.

When I first became saved, we used to sing a song at church called "Psalm 9." The first two verses from which that song is taken read, "I will tell of all Your wonders. I will be glad and exult in You" (NAS). When I sang those words, I sang them from the bottom of my heart and silently promised God that I would tell of His wonders. This book, in part, fulfills that promise.

CHAPTER ONE

Getting To Know Him

I believe the body of Christ desires to want to live for Christ. We want to know how to follow Christ while on earth. We want to be Christlike without being religious. We want to know how to be Christians in a world with unbelieving people and surrounded by evil. Sometimes that can be a daunting task. I know it has been for me.

We also want to know the process a person goes through in following Christ. We want to know if we are doing it "correctly." I don't know if I am doing things correctly, but I know this—I have purposed in my heart always to go forward. And when I fall down, I have determined in my heart that I am going to fall forward like those football players trying to gain an extra yard. I wish I could stand before you and say, "Gee, following God is a piece of cake!" Well, it's not. My flesh is constantly at war with what I know is right, which resists my moving forward. And we must persist against that which resists us. Struggling is part of the process. Most people, however, give up in the middle of a battle to search for some instant relief. That is why so many people go through cycles in their lives of always reliving a pattern.

Before we can break free of the cycles and answer the other issues, we first must have a desire to know God. We need to be aware that He wants to have a relationship with us. He already knows us; He knows every thought and every deed we have done. When I was first saved, my approach was simply this: Lord, I know you know everything already, so I am not going to keep anything from you, no matter how bad or ugly or dirty it may be. That opened a dialogue with a Father who loved me. I didn't keep anything back. Prayer is honesty.

Over twenty years ago, I embarked on the most meaningful, adventurous, warm, loving, and fulfilling relationship I have ever had. Never being one for fairy tales or romance stories, something radical happened in my heart that filled me with peace and acceptance that I had never experienced before. I had an encounter with the living God.

Partly because of my own personality, and partly because I didn't know any better, I just started talking to the Lord from my heart, sharing every detail of my life with Him. Innocently enough, I figured that He already knew everything anyway, so why hold back. Then one day I realized that He was talking to me!

Generally, I am a simple woman or rather a very simpleminded woman. My husband will second that. Small tasks like opening up the ironing board confound me. But I think God has a sense of humor and loves paradoxes, so He created the duckbill platypus and people like me. All joking aside, simplicity is of God. Paul says in Second Corinthians 11:3 (KJV), "But I fear, lest by any means, as the serpent beguiled Eve through his subtlety, so your minds should be corrupted from the simplicity that is in Christ." Too often, people, especially new believers, feel as if they need a degree in theology with emphasis in Greek and Hebrew before they can know Scriptures properly and then have relationship. As difficult as this is for many people to accept, knowing the Bible is not a substitute for the personal relationship to which God has called us. The Word of God is a who and not a what. The Word of God is the living Christ (John 1:1). We don't even have to know Greek or Hebrew to know Him. The simplicity of knowing Christ cuts across education and experience.

In the hit Broadway musical, *The King and I*, a scene is included in which the governess, Anna Leonowens, meets the king's children and sings the memorable song "Getting To Know You." The lyrics by Oscar Hammerstein II convey the hopes and process of relationship and the changes caused by that relationship.

This song, though secular, expresses my own desire to have a personal relationship with our heavenly Father through His Son, Jesus Christ, the King. In fact, it is a song that I sing to the King of Kings.

My desire to have a personal relationship with the King is a response to His desire for me to know Him. God is calling us to a place of getting to know Him in a more real, intimate way. And the results of this relationship, like in the song, will be that we come into a place of freedom and fewer burdens. To a dark world we will be a bright light set apart by love and joy. All of this is a result of the beautiful and new things we learn about Him day by day What a picture of our "King and I."

Somehow, due to our own dysfunctional relationships and to society, we have lost the simplicity of entering into His presence simply to be with Him. We struggle in our attempts to believe and receive His love. In our humanness, we have expectations of how God should relate to us. Always the encouraging Father, He has not given up on His kids. In every aspect of our lives, He is speaking to us, reaching out to us, touching us, and waiting for us to acknowledge and experience Him. God wants to reveal Himself to His children. The key is to recognize His presence in our lives and then respond.

God reveals Himself to us through our circumstances, our hopes and dreams, our gifts and talents, and the supernatural. Then it is up to us to respond through faith, obedience, humility, and love. The result will be the glory of His presence, the manifestation of His purpose, and the kingdom that is His plan. All of this begins with the desire for getting to know Him.

I spent most of my life not understanding that God wanted a personal relationship with me. Even though I believed in God, went to a traditional church, and read my Bible, I had missed out on something important—the intimacy of a personal relationship with Him, a God who cared about every aspect of my life, a God who wanted to communicate with me. I had difficulty comprehending that He wanted to talk to me. It's like a line from the movies in which the character says, "Are you talkin' to me?" Why on earth would He want to talk to me? Certainly there were more important, more entertaining, and more perfect people that He could talk to. But as I came to know Him and recognized the way He speaks to me, I came to understand that part of His divine plan was for me to share what He was doing in my life and who He is in my life. Personally, I felt He could have chosen someone better and more willing. Father God didn't agree. He chose me to share one little segment of His immeasurable being. So here I am, sharing the reality of Christ through daily living—applying the living Word to our twenty-first century thinking.

Jesus says in John 10:27 (KJV), "My sheep hear my voice, and I know them, and they follow me." Three parts comprise this verse. The sheep recognize the voice of God, which is a familiar voice. When some of my friends call me, I know who they are by the sound of their voice. They don't have to identify themselves, nor do I check the caller ID. That is familiarity born out of intimacy and time spent together. God wants us to be so familiar with His voice that we recognize Him when He is speaking to us.

The second part of the verse says that the Shepherd knows them. That indicates relationship. They know His voice and He knows theirs. He knows their character. He knows what they are going to do, and He is looking out for them.

The third part of this verse explains the outcome of this intimate relationship—the sheep follow this Good Shepherd. They go where He goes. They may not know why. They may not even know where they are going, but they go because He is good, loving, and kind. They do this because of mutual relationship and trust.

This verse is important because it is in the present tense. Christ's sheep still hear His voice because He is still speaking. He is alive. When He died on the cross, He arose from the dead and ascended into heaven to be with the Father. He then sent the Holy Spirit to be our Comforter and friend. In a society that is so willing to believe in the darkness and reality of witchcraft and Satanism, why aren't people more willing to believe in the One who defeated evil? Unfortunately, I know part of the answer: religion has distorted the view of God and who He is. We are too willing to fix our circumstances ourselves instead of allowing God to help us. We don't trust Him. He becomes a last resort instead of the first resource. Instead of allowing Him to work in our hearts, we allow Him to be just part of our minds.

But He is so much greater than our human minds. He is, after all, Creator of the universe. Jeremiah 33:3 (NKJV) says, "Call to Me, and I will answer you, and show you great and mighty things, which you do not know."

Throughout the Bible, we see the great men and women of God

having relationship and conversations with a God they knew intimately. Abraham and Moses were friends with God (James 2:23, Ex. 33:11). Isaiah, David, and Jeremiah talked honestly and openly about their feelings and struggles to a God who they knew would answer. They all knew they could call on Him with the assurance that He would respond and give them revelations they didn't know. He would offer them direction, answers, and friendship.

In times that are more modern, we know that George Washington Carver had this kind of relationship with the Creator. It is documented that in a conversation with God, he asked Him why He had made the peanut. The Lord proceeded to show him over 300 products that came from the little peanut. Another 150 uses came from the sweet potato. Through intimacy, God showed this man great and mighty things that he did not know.

God wants to have an intimate relationship with His people through His Son, Jesus Christ. Let me take that back. God wants to have an intimate relationship with all that He has created. Even if you don't know Him personally—even if you have never asked Him into your heart—God still loves you. He is waiting to be part of your life. He is waiting to be invited into your heart. He is on the outside looking in. But His desire is to be on the inside looking out.

When I pray, I don't say "God." I very rarely even say "Father." When I pray, He is "Daddy." Jesus referred to His Father as "Abba" (Mark 14:36), which is a term of endearment like "Daddy" or "Papa." So that is how He is for me. And He's not my buddy either, but He is my friend. There is a reverence and respect born out of an intimate relationship and knowledge of His position and authority. Yet, God, the Father, is my Daddy, and I am His child. He is not like earthly fathers because He is the perfect Father.

I remember talking to Him about this once. I have always had a good relationship with my earthly father, and the Lord and I were discussing it. Then the Lord asked me, "But weren't there things you wish your earthly father had done for you?"

I thought about it for a minute and then answered. "Daddy, I wish he had helped me focus more on my career and future. And I wish he could have told me what to wear on those days I couldn't make a decision." (That was important to me at the time.)

The Lord said, "I can do all those things and more."

When I pray, I expect that God wants to be with me and will respond. In childlike faith, I believe He created me because He wants to walk with me and talk with me. Sometimes I have to slow down to listen and to remember not to do all the talking. And this didn't happen overnight. Over time, I have learned how to tune in and hear Him.

When I was first saved, I heard a story that impacted me greatly. For me it epitomizes this relationship with the heavenly Father and how He wants me to see Him and respond to Him.

During the Cuban missile crisis, President John F. Kennedy was in the Oval Office surrounded by his team of advisors. It was a very tense time for our nation and especially for the President. All of a sudden, his little son, John-John, rushed through the door into the room looking for this father. In the middle of this crisis, President Kennedy stopped what he was doing, picked up his son, sat in his rocking chair, and held him. He gave his child all of his attention. He listened to him. He talked to him. Then John-John left, and the President went back to work.

Even if we never had that kind of earthly father, we do have it with our heavenly one. This is how I see my Father. I am always bursting in on Him. Being the loving, kind, gentle Father that He is, He stops what He is doing—for me. He loves me so much that He sent His only begotten Son to die on the cross—for me (John 3:16).

Revelation 4:11 (KJV) says, "Thou art worthy, O Lord, to receive glory and honour and power: for thou hast created all things, and for thy pleasure they are and were created." God is worthy. He is awesome. I love spending time with Him, and I was created to be a pleasure to Him. Sometimes I playfully tease Him and tell Him I am more than a pleasure; I am a source of amusement. I know He enjoys me as I enjoy my children. I know He shakes His head as He considers the fact that He made a woman who in most cases is quite bright and intelligent, but can't for the life of her pump gas. He enjoys the fact that at my age I still slide down the sliding board at the park, even when my kids aren't around—especially when my kids aren't around. But He also enjoys the fact that He is the first one I run to when my feelings are hurt or when I am angry and frustrated.

Several years ago, my family forgot my birthday, and I was hurt. I felt unappreciated and lonely. The next day was Sunday, and I was so sad that I stayed home from church while the rest of the family went to the service. I sat on the floor of the bedroom and cried pathetically to the Lord. And I let Him know that I was mad at Him too. "You are so real to me," I said, sobbing. "You created me and You didn't get me anything either. Even You forgot me."

Two days later, my friend Kim and I spent the day together. She picked me up in her car, and we just rode around and had some fun. On the way back to my house, she became serious. "Gael," she said, "in the bag between the seats is a gift for you. I didn't have a chance to wrap it."

I reached for the bag and as I unfolded the gift, Kim said, "Oh, and one more thing—the Father said it's from Him. Happy Birthday."

At those words, I started to cry uncontrollably. I hadn't told a soul about my pity party with the Lord. He hadn't forgotten me after all.

God does care about what matters to me. And more and more I care about what matters to Him. Ultimately this journey is not about me—it's about Him.

CHAPTER TWO

Hunger Pains

The Lord showed me something recently about desiring Him. He said there is a lack of hunger for Him and the things of God. Having been anorexic for many years, I understand that disorder. I never had hunger pains. I didn't have the mechanism that told me when to eat. It had been suppressed by years of not eating regularly or in a healthy manner. One day when I was praying for an anorexic woman who needed help, the Lord told me that I had been healed because I was hungry for Him. I immediately started praying that this woman would be hungry for the Lord. I knew that as she hungered for more of Him, she would desire to know Him, please Him, and believe Him—and then she would obey Him. Her desire and obedience to the Lord would bring healing to her life because as a good Father, He would show her what is necessary to bring that healing.

But anorexics don't want to be hungry. They don't like that word. Then one day I was with my oldest daughter at the mall. She was getting something to eat at the food court when she asked me if I wanted anything. I told her I wasn't hungry. Then I smelled the food. The aroma of the goodies stirred something in me, and suddenly I was hungry. The Lord started to speak to me, saying, "The Church is spiritually anorexic. It is getting full by living on junk food. It needs the meat of my Word. Pray that the fragrance of my presence will make them hungry for Me." And that is what I prayed and still pray.

The Church's appetite for God has been suppressed by a poor diet. We have been fed junk food. We have no hunger pains. We don't even know how to feed ourselves. If you don't have a compelling desire to know God more, ask Him. Stop right now and pray.

God, I don't have a hunger for You, but I want to feel that desire. I want to know You. I want to get to know You. Please make me hungry for You. I don't want junk food or substitutions for the real thing anymore. I want a healthy diet of Your presence and the Living Word. Thank you, Father. I love you.

As we become hungry for Him, we will experience the glory of His presence. And boy do things get exciting! Like the song "Getting To Know You," everything is beautiful and new. We see everything from a different point of view; we see it from God's perspective.

Of course, this is a process that is part of the plan. A few years ago, some friends of mine brought a sick friend to see me for prayer. I have been praying with this group of women off and on for ten years. We all attend different churches, enjoy each other's company, and get together when a need presents itself.

That day I learned that a woman named Donna had cancer. She had struggled with breast cancer and was still fighting the fight. The prognosis wasn't good, and she had two sons to take care of and support. As soon as I met her, I just loved her. She was precious. My heart ached for her pain and suffering. We all sat on the floor together and started to offer our petitions to the Lord. One of my friends prayed for God to heal Donna if it was His will. At that moment, I heard the Lord say to me, "My will? I died for this!" I had never heard Him so indignant before. He continued, "Stop this prayer. I am going to heal her. I could heal her in less than a blink of an eye, but I am more interested in the process."

Wow! God had given me such insight into His plan. He cares about the process. He could perform miracles immediately and suddenly, but He is interested in the growth that we will experience. The Israelites could have left Egypt sooner, but God had purpose in the process. They could have wandered eleven days instead of forty years, but there was a reason for the delay. Sometimes the trial is a result of our own disobedience and hardheadedness. But other times it is all God, and He wants to teach us something more about Him or us. Sometimes in the process, the garbage in our lives comes to the surface to be cleaned off by Him.

In the commotion is often when we have divine encounters that lead us to the next place in our lives. Consequently, we can be in His will but still go through difficult times and struggle. Moses was in God's will, but he had to come against an obstinate Pharaoh and then lead a stiff-necked group of people. The Israelites were in God's will, yet they faced wars in the Promised Land; and so will we.

When Donna was going through another medical battle, the Lord told me that I should not doubt Him. He said, "I am healing her stitch by stitch like a beautiful quilt."

The next day I started a new Bible study, and the lesson was about one of the definitions of the word heal, which The New Strong's Exhaustive Concordance of the Bible says means, "to mend (by stitching)." And in the room where we met was a beautiful quilt. Later I told Donna (who is a quilter) what God had showed me. She was so encouraged and uplifted to continue the fight. She had hope. She had faith. She became acquainted with the living God who cared about every part of her, a God who is in control and has a plan. He is interested in the process of her total healing—physical as well as spiritual and emotional. Donna went through a time of remission and recovery, living and ministering for several productive years before passing away. Her amazing testimony included the faith she acquired and the joy that she walked in, all because of the process. God restored His little girl, and He was glorified in the process. Every person who ever met Donna and saw how she lived saw the Lord in her. She lived fully and faithfully. When Donna went to be with the Lord, two women in our church had a vision of her joyfully dancing before Him. She was perfected and whole. My prayer is that this will make you hungry for more of Him.

CHAPTER THREE

Can You Hear Me Now?

Some of you might be wondering how God speaks to us. This is not a book about how to hear from God. Some very good books deal specifically with that topic. But we have to acknowledge that God does speak. He communicates with His creation. A look at the Bible shows ordinary people who not only heard from God but who also had entire conversations with Him. Abraham, Moses, David, Jeremiah, Isaiah, Elijah, and Paul are just a few of the people with human weaknesses that all talked with God. I believe God converses as we do. Genesis 1:3 reads, "And God said, Let there be light: and there was light" (emphasis added). God spoke and things happened. We see Him speaking throughout the Word.

This is still true today. God continues to speak. There is a generation of Enochs that God is calling to Himself. They are His friends, fellowshipping and loving Him for who He is, not just what He does. They know their King. To hear Him, we just need to tune into His frequency. It's like dialing into a radio station; sometimes we get static, and sometimes the signal comes in loud and clear. We need to know how to tune in and listen, and we need to know what to do when we get static. So the issue is not that God speaks; it is how we hear. God speaks in many ways to keep us on our toes, which requires training and mistakes. Because if we are honest, we do glean more from our errors than we do from any other type of learning. The Lord told me once that mistakes were already worked into the plan for that very reason.

When I write, "God told me" or "the Lord said" or "He showed me," those are broad ways of saying that God communicated with me.

But the forms of that delivery come in many ways. He speaks audibly, through impressions, with the inner voice of the Holy Spirit, in dreams, in visions, and through Scripture. He can use unbelievers, believers, circumstances, movies, books, or whatever is in our lives to speak to us. His ways of imparting messages to us are endless. We just have to learn to hear and recognize His voice. For example, I can communicate nonverbally with my children by giving them a particular look. Or I can convey my feelings through tears or laughter. I can also express myself through cooking, art, and music. God also has a variety of ways of speaking with us.

People don't have to hear from God in the same manner that I do to have a personal relationship with Him. God reveals Himself to each individual in a way that can be heard and understood in that person's life. He just wants to be involved and recognized in our lives.

God's communication with me started many years ago when I was living a sinful life. As I said earlier, I had gone to a traditional church and believed in God, but I didn't believe God. I didn't know Him; I didn't have that personal relationship with Him. It's like saying, "I know Oprah Winfrey is a real, live person, but I don't know her personally."

Anyway, my personal life was falling apart when I called a friend who offered to pray for me. When he started to pray, it was as though a light bulb turned on over my head like in some cartoon and I thought, *I'm going to pray for myself.* I don't even remember what my friend prayed, but I know that as soon as I got off the phone, I went into the bathroom, got on my knees in front of the toilet, and said, "Jesus, if You're real, help me. I can't do it myself anymore." At this moment, in what I can only describe as a lightning bolt going through me, I was transformed. And immediately I heard, "Go and sin no more." I remember thinking, *That's in the Bible.*

Now I know this sounds dramatic, and I know that this doesn't happen to everyone. But God had to be big with me. He had to get my attention. The effect is the same whether we accept Christ quietly in our pews or before a million people at a crusade; the Holy Spirit comes into our hearts and resides. The rest is up to us as to how we will respond and how much we will let God direct our lives.

Since my traditional church did not prepare me for this kind of encounter, I just went along with what I was experiencing. Some of you might be thinking, *Now Gael, that can be dangerous. Feelings and emotions are of the flesh.* Oh, yes, I suppose it could be if you were praying with impure motives or dallying about with someone other than God. But my heart was aching, I was searching for God, and what was happening to me was real.

When I came out of the bathroom, my girlfriend who was visiting asked, "What happened to you?" I told her that I had just become a Christian. The transformation was so immediate and evident she knew something had changed while I was in the bathroom!

I had heard of born-again Christians, and now I knew I was one of them. Again, my traditional upbringing had not prepared me for this. When some Christians have an experience, it can be like getting into a swimming pool. They go in one foot at a time, slowly wading out until they are in over their heads immersed in the Holy Spirit. Not me. I dove off the deep end without being able to swim. But again, it had to be that way so that there was no backing out on my part. God knows how to reach each individual.

After my salvation experience, I immediately started praying to a God who was real. I told Him, "I don't know how to pray using 'thee' and 'thou,' so I'm just going to talk to you like I talk to everybody else." Later on, when I knew His voice more clearly, He told me how much that meant to Him and how long He had waited to hear me speak so casually and intimately. And for some reason my traditional upbringing had me believing that God still spoke in King James English. But God doesn't because I don't. He just wants to hear my voice speaking to Him naturally. Thank goodness. I talk to Him as I talk to my family and friends, and He loves it!

I relate all of this to say that God wants us to talk to Him. Sometimes I'll jokingly ask Him if He wants a cup of coffee. I invite Him to sit with me on the love seat. He is so real and personal. When I pray, I know He wants to be with me, just as I want to be with Him.

But I have made wrong assumptions in how God speaks to others. My husband doesn't "hear" as I do. One night I was frustrated because we needed a word from God on an issue. The Lord wasn't speaking to me about it, and I was concerned that Mike wasn't hearing. I was walking through the dining room when the Lord spoke. He said, "Mike doesn't hear from Me like you do, yet he faithfully prays every day knowing he probably won't hear anything. He is faithful." I immediately repented to the Lord and to Mike.

God discloses His infinite depth in countless ways. For example, He speaks to Mike through science fiction and flying. I have no interest in either of those subjects. The Lord told me once, "I can't talk to you through science fiction, but I can with Mike. He can relate to Me and understand things on that level that you just can't." And boy, is that the truth. How exciting that God can do that with us! He can reveal His uniqueness to us and through us. That's why I love hearing testimonies and reading biographies of God's people. The same story is never told twice. Repeats or reruns don't take place with God.

But there are common ways to hear and communicate with God. The first and foremost way God speaks is through Scripture. God doesn't need to say many things again because He has already made it clear in the pages of His Word. I know not to steal or kill because the Bible says so. Many times by speaking Scriptures out loud, God has brought peace and comfort to my life. Other times He has guided me to a particular Scripture to give me a specific promise.

When my oldest son, Adam, went away to college, I grieved; I missed him so much. I was reading *The Living Bible* when the following verse jumped off the page at me: "So I am all the more anxious to get him back to you again, for I know how thankful you will be to see him, and that will make me happy and lighten all my cares. Welcome him in the Lord with great joy, and show your appreciation" (Phil. 2:28-29 TLB).

That was God speaking specifically to me. How did I know? Something connected inside of me. My heart quickened. It was so spontaneous. Tears welled up in my eyes. But you know what I loved? I loved that God was showing His heart towards me. He cared about what mattered to me. He cared that I was missing my son. And not only did He show me His heart, He gave me direction as to how to welcome him.

God speaks in many ways. I have only heard Him speak audibly once in my life. I had slept in one morning and heard a booming voice say, "Gael." Then I heard it again. I didn't recognize the voice, but it was a man who obviously knew me. Silly me, I buried myself under the covers. I figured that if I hid deeply enough, whoever was there would think I had left the house without making my bed. Then I heard the voice for a third time. I knew it wasn't just some man in my house. I knew who it was. My mind raced to the passage in the Bible in which Samuel heard a voice that sounded so familiar that he thought it was Eli before that teacher pointed him in the right direction. It was God.

I got up and humbly stood before the Lord. I couldn't speak. But I knew that God was literally calling me out (from hiding under the covers) and into His presence.

Hearing from God audibly was a onetime thing for me so far. Recently though, my youngest son, Max, heard his name called twice while he was in bed. He thought it was one of his brothers talking to him. When he called to his brother to ask what he wanted, Alex replied that he had not said a word. Then when Max heard it the third time, he too remembered the story of Samuel. I asked Max what he thought God wanted. He said, "I think God wants me to speak to Him."

I believe more people will start hearing God's voice audibly. And isn't it interesting that Samuel was at rest when he heard from God? As we maintain a place of rest and quiet, we will hear the Lord more clearly. We will hear the still, small voice (1 Kings 19:12).

Another way I hear from God is through impressions. This is where I make a lot of mistakes. Hearing the true voice of God, though, is a training process. And God doesn't always speak to me the same way. He wants me to look and listen for Him in all things. Since relying on impressions is emotionally based, I have to be careful that what I am thinking or feeling is backed by Scripture. I also receive counsel from my husband and others in authority that I trust. But I have found that when I don't go with my gut instinct, I usually make my biggest mistakes. And if I don't have peace, I don't do anything.

The most common way I hear from the Lord is through an inner voice. I have had to make many, many errors to discern between what is God, is the enemy, and what is me. And I will continue to make missteps. But in this season of my life, this is how I usually hear from God.

This is also how I heard Him that very first time in the bathroom. It was an inner voice in my heart speaking to me. It was not in my mind; it was in my heart. But the voice was so clear. However, I always have to make sure that what I am hearing is in the Bible or has a biblical precedent; and if it isn't or doesn't, I discard it or ponder it for a time until God reveals it to me. This causes me to dig deeper and seek Him. Sometimes what I hear is not what I want to hear.

Some people hear from God through their dreams. Joseph was considered a dreamer (Gen. 37). God spoke to others in the Bible through dreams too, and He still speaks through dreams today. I dream all the time. Again, I've had to learn what is from God (those significant dreams) and what isn't. Some are profound messages from above, and some are junk mail. I've had some very poignant dreams giving me direction. Joseph, Jesus' earthly father, had those kinds of dreams. I had one in which I was told not to sign a legal paper. I didn't. In another dream, I was told I would receive exactly one thousand dollars and instructed to put half of it into "God's account" to be used as the Lord directed. The other half we could use as we wished. I told Mike the dream when I awakened. Thankfully, I am married to a man who also hears from God, even though God communicates with him differently. We both knew this dream was significant. A few days later, we received a check for exactly one thousand dollars in the mail. It was a total surprise, and it confirmed my dream. Throughout the next year, we used God's account to bless people as we were led. Only later did we realize that there were times when we could have used that money. But it never, ever crossed our minds to use it for ourselves.

I have had other dreams in which God helped me work out fears and struggles. After a series of bad nights with uncomfortable dreams, I complained to the Lord. He replied, "Well, we can do this while you are asleep or while you are awake." I chose to work through this particular issue while I was asleep.

I don't understand all my dreams either. To be honest, the fact that I dream so consistently without understanding them frustrates me. I have asked for a gift of interpretation like Joseph and Daniel had, but God has not given it to me—yet. But dreaming as I do keeps me before the Lord continually seeking Him for understanding.

God also speaks through visions (Joel 2:28-29; Acts 2:17-18). For me these have multiplied over the years. I have them for myself and for others. I like getting dreams and visions because I can't create them myself. I don't have that kind of imagination. So when I see something, I have no doubt as to what I see. I just record it or speak it out if appropriate at that time. But I don't always understand what I see. I have had to learn not to try to offer an interpretation when the Lord has not given it to me. That is just one of those pitfalls in the learning process. All of this takes time and practice. God puts us in situations where we have to learn and lean on Him for understanding, wisdom, and revelation. And I am always learning.

God does speak through other people, saved and unsaved. If God can speak through a donkey (Num. 22:28), He can surely speak through people. So I listen for Him when I am talking to others too. Many times He has used my children to say the words I need to hear or feel. Once I told the Lord that I wished I could feel Him hug me. I needed that comfort so much that day. When Adam, who was in fifth grade at the time, came home from school, he ran up to me, threw his arms around me in an overpowering way, and told me how much he loved me. In that moment I heard the Lord say, "That's from Me." I loved it.

Sometimes the most difficult way for me to hear from God right away is in my circumstances. Conditions might appear to be so bad that, at first, I can't tell if it is Him or not. When we have experienced financial problems, I sometimes have had to wait for the dust to settle and for my immediate emotions to be out of the way to see that God was teaching me a new lesson on trust or faith.

God will use whatever is in our lives to speak to us to reveal Himself, His love, and His desires for us. The clarity and frequency with which He speaks to us depends on our willingness and desire to have Him in our lives and then to follow Him.

CHAPTER FOUR

Did I Really See That?

I was walking down the street to my apartment years ago when I heard the Lord speak to me. He told me to go back to the dumpster I had just passed and talk to the man there. I thought I was hearing things, so I tried to continue walking down the sidewalk. But I couldn't take a step. Something invisible was in front of me that kept me from moving forward. I then turned around and went back to the dumpster.

There, digging in the trash, was an older man. He was wearing clothes that one would expect of someone who was digging in the dumpster. I didn't know what to say, so I asked the Lord, "What should I do?"

He replied, "Tell him that I love him."

So I turned to the man at the dumpster and said, "The Lord loves you."

The man looked at me with a funny look and said, "That's nice."

I had a feeling that there was more to this but was hoping I could go home when the Lord said, "Say it again."

I looked at the man again and said, "Jesus loves you."

The man at the dumpster didn't miss a beat and said in a voice that made me question his mental faculties, "She does?"

Now by this time I was a little frustrated, and I just didn't know what God wanted me to do. I asked the Lord again to give me direction, and He did. "Touch him," He said.

One last time I turned to the man, reached out, and touched him. "Jesus loves you," I said with my hand on his arm.

This time the response was different. This time I was looking into the face of someone with the sweetest smile and the gentlest demeanor. With a direct look at me, he replied with a strong, firm voice, "I know He does. Thank you."

I walked away from the man and the dumpster. This time I had no problem in reaching my door. Nothing impeded me. I was shaking and somewhat bewildered. I knew I had just encountered something or someone significant. The verse that came to my mind was Hebrews 13:2 (KJV), "Be not forgetful to entertain strangers for thereby some have entertained angels unawares."

A hunger for the supernatural is unmistakable in our society. Just look at the prevalence of television shows, movies, and books about the supernatural. Yet in the church, as soon as anyone talks about something paranormal, we are carried off to the loony bin of the mind. Now that is not to express that I don't struggle with feeling as if my life is just a little crazy at times. I can't believe that these events happen to me, but they do. I told the Lord a long time ago that I wanted to go as far as the Bible goes. There isn't any denying that the Lord used angels to set Peter free from prison. An angel spoke to Mary about her future. God uses angels. The Lord still uses angels to help us, guide us, protect us, and convey God's loving care to us.

One night Mike and I were upstairs in our room when we heard a knock at the front door. Mike went to answer it and was gone for some time. I sensed that something was wrong, but I waited for him.

When Mike came back, he told me he had some bad news. A woman was downstairs with Sydney, our little Yorkshire terrier. Unbeknownst to us, he had escaped from the house. She had seen him get hit by a car on the main road. The woman saw that Sydney was confused, so she followed him home. She wanted to make sure that we knew he was hurt, so she had knocked on the door.

I ran downstairs to my little dog. The woman was pleasant, young, and pretty. Mike and I examined Sydney, who was in serious condition. When we looked up, the woman was gone. She had disappeared! We looked out onto the street, but there was no sign of her. The way our house was situated, we would have been able to see someone walking for blocks.

Later that night, we had to have Sydney put to sleep. I was hysterical. Mike called our veterinarian, who also happened to be an elder in our church. John spoke gently to me while I sobbed uncontrollably. He said, "Gael, God loves you so much that He sent an angel to make sure Sydney got home so you wouldn't worry."

I knew in my heart that he was right. That woman was an angel. That is why she disappeared. God was not only looking out for me; He was looking out for Sydney too. God was showing me an aspect of His active love in my life.

Years later, there was another knock at the front door. A man was standing there and asked Mike if we could spare some food. We usually don't bring strangers directly into our house. We have to be careful because we live in a rough neighborhood, but Mike invited this man into our home. This particular Saturday night we were eating very late. We were having a simple spaghetti dinner. The man joined us and we started to talk. We even wondered if he had been drinking. After the meal, we asked if we could pray for him. He said yes. While we prayed, we noticed a change in him. He looked at us with clear eyes and with a clear voice asked if he could now pray for us. We said yes. He then laid hands on us and prayed a blessing over us. He left our house, and we never saw him again.

Again, like before, we knew we had entertained an angel. We have strangers come to the house all the time. We feed, clothe, hand out blankets, and pray for them. Mike has even washed the laundry of the homeless and cut their hair. But this man was different.

Once I sensed a very large angel next to my bed. I didn't see him physically, but I knew he was there. I asked the Lord if the angel loved me. The Lord said, "No, but he does respect you. He can only love Me." That was such a revelation. While we are not to make worshipping the angels a religion, unlike the Sadducees (Acts 23:8), we can accept that God uses them in our lives.

One particularly bad night in the neighborhood, I went upstairs to look out the window. I saw two huge angels standing guard in front of the house like sentries. I cried out to the Lord, "There are two angels out front. What are they doing there?"

At that very moment, a car came down the street. In the back seat, a hand was pointing a gun out of a darkened window. Four shots rang out in front of my home. Not one bullet went through the house. The next morning I found four 9-mm bullet casings in the front yard. Those angels protected us, and God allowed me to see them at work. He was letting me know that Psalm 91:11 (AMP) is true for today, "For He will give His angels [especial] charge over you to accompany and defend and preserve you in all your ways [of obedience and service]."

I am not the only one in the family who has seen angels. My oldest daughter, Brook, was just a preteen when she flew to see some relatives. She wasn't happy about flying alone. She boarded the plane and quietly asked God to help her. When she looked out the window, she saw an angel on the wing waving to her. Brook waved back and had peace the entire flight.

When our twins were little, we would watch their little heads bob in unison to something unseen to the rest of us. Together their eyes would track something only they were able to see. We knew they were tracking the movement of angels over them.

But the supernatural is not just about angels. I was driving home from a long day trip one time when I realized I hadn't eaten all day. To have the strength to make the rest of the trip, I knew I had to eat. I saw a fast-food restaurant up ahead and decided to stop. But I didn't even have enough change for the dollar menu. I counted out the coins in my hand when all of a sudden the pennies and nickels changed to dimes and quarters. Fuzziness came over my brain because my mind could not comprehend what had occurred in my hand. Later I jokingly told the Lord that next time I will have to believe for the regular menu. And you know what? I believe He does want me to believe for greater miracles.

I have had other supernatural encounters that were not always of God. Fear and darkness accompanied them. That aspect is also very real. I pray the supernatural of God's kingdom would become natural to us. We need a mindset that allows God to come and do whatever He wants, however He wants. I want to see the presence of God be so real that His supernatural power would be manifested as it was in the Bible. Let's see some burning bushes. Let's see the waters separate. Let's blow the trumpets and see walls come tumbling down. I am in favor of seeing my loved ones raised from the dead if it is not their time. How about it? Do we believe God is who He says He is and that He can do what He says He can do? The hunger for the supernatural in our society is real. But the void will continue to be filled with darkness and evil if we don't allow God to show us His reality and His power.

The miracles that take place on other continents happen because the people accept the supernatural. I asked God once why He doesn't do more miracles and healings in this country. He said, "You try to do everything yourselves. You go to the doctors first. Then you go to the government. Then you steal and take it for yourselves. People come to Me as a last resort instead of a first recourse." If we will go to God first and trust Him in the way He wants to work in our lives, the supernatural will become the natural.

CHAPTER FIVE

Flakiness Is for Pie Crusts

By now, you may be thinking that I have lost a few screws along the way. I see things, I hear things, and I perceive things. And we haven't even gotten to the good stuff yet. Well, for the record, many times I've felt as though I were losing it. I thought I was crazy myself. Do I walk around in a constant state of always seeing and hearing things? No! But I do try to keep my eyes and ears open to what God is doing.

Not long ago, a pastor's wife, a woman I love and admire, was talking and prepared me for something difficult by saying, "Gael, I don't want to hurt you, but . . ."

Well, right there you know that it's time to brace yourself to get hit by a truck.

"You are so eccentric."

Me? Eccentric? Oh, that did hurt. Immediately I started to defend myself and tell her all the reasons I wasn't eccentric. I told her I was logical. I tried to convince her that I'm emotionally stable. Then I gave her the minute version of my resume. It didn't work.

After I hung up the phone, I went to the Lord and said, "Daddy, that hurt. I don't want to be considered eccentric."

He fired back at me, "John the Baptist, Ezekiel, and Isaiah were all considered eccentric."

Oh, that puts me in great company—a guy who is known for eating locusts and honey, another who lies on his side for 430 days, and still another one who goes naked for three years. But I understood what the Lord was really saying; nothing is wrong with being called eccentric when it is because of Him.

Some people say that I live in the clouds, but I like being in the Lord's presence. Sometimes He has to tell me to be practical again—you know, like cook and clean. For the record, I want you to know I really am a very logical person.

So why address this topic? Because it is important to explain that goofiness in spirituality is not of God. Hearing from God is not a license to be flaky. Flakiness is for pie crusts. God wants to communicate with us, but He also wants us to be responsible with what He tells us to do. That requires training, submission, and accountability. It involves humility, and it means making mistakes.

I've made a lot of mistakes. I will continue to make many more. That is how we learn. To equip the saints, churches must provide safe places where people can fail.

I was in a church where we experienced a season of deliverance. That was a crazy time. We made a major error by focusing on the demonic rather than the Deliverer. Good lesson.

One church was seeking to appeal to man rather than seeking the presence of the Holy Spirit. Not a good idea.

I was in a church where people were more interested in being leaders than being like Christ. Very bad idea.

Another time we found we were worshipping "worship" and not the One to be worshipped. Big mistake.

In my personal life, I gave a word to the pastor before a staff meeting. Horrible timing! The pastor was so shaken up that he cancelled the meeting before it ever started. And even though the word was right on, the timing wasn't. Timing is crucial.

I once pushed Mike to pursue a job at a company. A friend of his hand carried his resume to the human resources department, even though my husband knew he was not qualified. The friend got in hot water for doing it. Mike was embarrassed, and I was ashamed. The Lord showed me that I pulled a Sarah. Like her, I did not wait on God's timing, nor did I honor my husband. Like Sarah, I took matters into my own hands to try to produce the outcome that would benefit us. I was seriously wrong.

Other times I have made presumptions about how God was going to work and how something would come to pass. Wrong. I have perceived things about people that I later found were totally incorrect. I have misunderstood situations and circumstances and misread them completely. Wrong. Wrong. Wrong.

I have at times expected God to revolve around me rather than me revolve around His Son. I have strived at times to move forward with God when I should have rested in Him. I have spoken when I should have been quiet. I have been quiet when I should have spoken. Each of these lessons was painful. And I confronted many, many more. But discipline is God's gentle way of pointing us in the right direction, if only we will accept it. I could have rebelled against authority. I could have walked away from God. However, as hard as it was, I chose to accept what God had to tell me and to watch Him lovingly restore me,

The best way to avoid flakiness is to make sure that what you are doing lines up with Scripture. Go to people in authority, people whom you trust that have wisdom and discernment. Wait on God for timing. Learn from your mistakes and from everyone else's. Be humble. Trust God for the outcome. Understand though, that it is not easy.

Once I received a call from a man who was very arrogant with me. I could feel myself putting up a defensive wall. I remembered what the Lord had told me when I put up walls of mistrust at a new church. He said quite casually, "I never had any walls up." As I remembered what He said, He spoke again, "Go lower." He was telling me to humble myself, let down those defensive walls, and go lower than this prideful man. I obeyed and submitted, listening with openness to what this man was saying without responding to his attitude. That night, the man called me back and behaved differently. He came to our house and blessed us in a powerful way. By listening to God and responding appropriately, I avoided a potential problem and received a blessing. By being humble, a mistake was avoided.

And sometimes I was right and everyone else was wrong, but the results were still the same: I had to submit, wait, and watch God lovingly restore my wounded heart. Oh, those times were difficult too.

One time a pastor became upset with me for something I said. For a year, the Lord kept telling me that the situation was not really about me; rather, it was between the pastor and Him. But I was caught in the middle, and I didn't like it. I told the Lord I would repent, that I would stand in front of the church if necessary. The Lord kept saying no. After thirteen months, I heard the Lord say, "Come out of the cave."

I knew the reference in 1 Kings 19 when Elijah is hiding in a cave. During those thirteen months, I could barely walk into church with my head up. I was so devastated. My relationship with a pastor who was also my friend was destroyed. I grieved. The Lord told me to believe Him in this situation and to forgive the pastor for the way he was treating me. And then He told me that the pastor might never realize what he had done to me. He asked me if I was prepared for that. I told Him I wasn't sure. I wanted reconciliation and restoration.

Then the Lord asked me something that I will never forget: "Do you want me to tell you about all of your mistakes?"

"No."

"Forgive him. Shake it off. Believe Me. And consider this—sometimes what feels like rejection is My protection."

So we're going to make mistakes. We're going to misunderstand. We're going to be misunderstood. We may even be flaky as we test the waters. We may even be right, though others think we are wrong. How do we persevere in pursuing Him? We must look at God's perspective.

Noah got drunk. Abraham lied. Jacob cheated. Moses killed a man. David committed adultery. The list continues. These people were redeemable. They were valuable. And so are we.

When a famous manuscript written by Ernest Hemingway was first published, the typesetter made a mistake in the printing. That error made the manuscript a collector's item. The mistake made it valuable.

That is how God sees us. Our mistakes, our humanity, and our lack of perfection make us valuable to Him. The men from the Bible listed above turned their hearts towards God. In some cases, we know they repented. In other cases, their actions are never mentioned again. But God's plans for them continued.

What God is looking for from us is a response. He told me once that He was going to make Himself known in my city—not because of anything we did, but by how we responded. His exact words were, "I am coming to Sanford, not because of anything you do, but because of how you respond." Those responses are not always the big progress that everyone sees but the small steps of obedience in everyday conduct.

My husband and I were visiting an intercessory prayer group one time that was rather immature. I was very uncomfortable with what I felt, so I went to the Lord and asked Him about it. He showed me little children who were bringing their clay ashtrays and dandelions to Him. They were bringing whatever they could in the only ways they knew—so far. He told me they were so sincere in what they were doing that He loved it. Immediately, my heart changed towards the group, and the Holy Spirit came in power. Then the leader asked my husband and me to pray for the group. When my heart lined up with God's perspective, He was able to move, and we were all blessed. I could have been a detriment to what God wanted because my heart was not one with His, and again I would have prevented a blessing.

If we justify our behavior and our feelings, and we refuse to submit to the Lord and to others, we can prevent the Holy Spirit from moving without encumbrance. Our response must be to do the will of God His way. Moses paid a price for not operating God's way. He was not allowed to enter the Promised Land. To this day, I still cry when I read the passage of how Moses was only allowed to see the Promised Land from Mount Nebo (Deut. 32:49-51). I realize that the line between walking God's way and mine is very fine.

Obtaining God's perspective on situations is vital. To stop and ask God to show us something takes so little time. If we do this, we will avoid many problems. Keep in mind that God will allow us to go through certain circumstances to experience for ourselves that we can be taken to a new place with Him. Our society so desperately wants to be perfect. We look at mistakes as failure, and failure is a bad word. For Christians we sometimes think that to be perfect means to be without fault or without sin, when actually it means to be complete. It is a process.

Mike had a dream one night in which he was told to obtain his real estate license. We both knew it was from God, but I was hesitant to accept it. I saw real estate as one step up from selling used cars. (I have since repented for both thoughts.) A month later, I ran into someone who told me that God was moving him into real estate and how he was being blessed. I knew this was a divine appointment from God. So I went home to Mike and confessed my feelings to him. I told him God was showing me that I needed to support him on this career change.

Mike started real estate school and did very well. In the middle of it, though, his mother unexpectedly died. We were gone for eleven days, and he missed several classes of a very intensive course. He continued with the course and missed the cutoff to take the state board by a few points. He was devastated. He was humiliated too because he had shared with the whole class that he was taking the course because of a dream in which God had spoken to him. But he went up to the teacher and told her he would be back to take it again.

When he came home, we cried. We just couldn't understand what had happened. Mike had been obedient to what we both felt God was telling him to do. But he had failed. How could he fail when God was in it? Had we missed God?

After a few days, when the emotional pain began to recede, the Lord showed us something. He told us that He doesn't see failure as we do. The real test was in Mike's response to what he knew God had instructed him to do. Mike's first response was to say he was going to try again. To God that was success, not failure. It still brings tears to my eyes to see that circumstance from God's perspective.

But it gets better. Mike took the course again. While he was in the course, he learned that his company was closing its doors. This time he passed the course and the state board. He acquired his real estate license six days before his job came to an end. Because Mike stayed with the company until it closed, he received a severance package. If he had passed the course the first time, he would have left the company without any benefits at all. God knew what He was doing. Mike had heard correctly, and we had learned a valuable lesson.

CHAPTER SIX

I'm Following As Closely As I Can

Returning again to John 10:27 (KJV) we read, "My sheep hear my voice, and I know them, and they follow me." Following God is one of the requirements and one of the benefits of hearing from God. I have seen a progression of both in my life. As I have continued to obey God, I have heard His voice and seen Him move with increasing clarity and frequency. But some of what He has required has been substantial and the process bewildering at times.

One of the biggest challenges we ever faced took place in 1993 when we were living in Colorado Springs, Colorado. We had a full life with four children and two dogs. It was late spring and I was getting ready to clean the house, but I didn't feel like cleaning the house. What I really wanted to do was pack. I wanted to pack up the entire house.

The next day I tried to clean again but was stopped by this over-whelming desire to pack. I went to the Lord and asked Him what was happening. Why didn't I want to clean? I am one of those people who like to clean, so what I was experiencing was new. And the added dimension of wanting to pack was confusing; I actually saw myself taking down pictures and putting things in boxes.

The only comment the Lord made was to say that things were going to happen fast. And He was not kidding. Events unfolded daily. Two days later, our landlord called to say that he wanted to sell the house we were renting. Then Mike came home and said that the company he worked for was moving to Chicago and not taking any employees. I started to pray with excitement and anticipation. I just knew something BIG was about to happen.

That Saturday our landlord called back to ask us if we wanted to buy the house. He was offering it to us at a very, very low price. It was a five bedroom house with two full baths, a big country kitchen, living room, workroom, and a huge family room. Even though Mike was losing his job, we knew the Lord would provide him with another one. To own a home was one of the greatest desires of our hearts.

I went to my prayer closet to pray. In this case, the prayer closet was a small bathroom. I sat on the floor and asked God what to do. The Lord said, "You are moving. Don't buy this house because I am going to give you a house beyond your expectations."

Now being who I am, my first thought was to skip the moving part, and let's talk about this house. "Daddy," I said, "do you know what kind of house I want?"

"Yes," He replied, "you want one with a porch, a deck, and lots of windows."

Even I hadn't thought of those things, but I knew He was right. I did want them.

"Lord, will we be in our new house by the time Brook graduates in a few weeks? Because you know we have company coming, and it would sure be nice to be in a different place."

"Daughter, you are mooooving."

Uh, oh, I thought. *I don't like this. I don't like the way He said moving.* We lived in beautiful Colorado Springs. We were attending a great church, and I was teaching college. But very quickly my mind started working. One of my students had just offered to help me get a horse. She was going to board it for free. Maybe we were moving outside of town to Black Forest to be near my future horse.

Now isn't this just like us mere mortals? We hear a little bit of something, and off go our imaginations. And my agenda too. I wanted to be in a house in a few weeks, staying close to my church and near that new horse that I didn't even own yet.

But there was a part of me that was shutting down. There was something I didn't want to hear. I didn't want to talk about moving. I wanted to hear about that new house, but something inside of me said I wasn't going to like the moving part too much. So I ended the conversation. It was a typical kid's response. I put my fingers in my ears. I didn't want to hear any more.

But God wasn't done talking.

As I prepared to leave the bathroom, the phone rang. It was my friend Manuela. "Get over here right away. I have a word for you from the Lord."

Oh, no, I thought. What could He possibly say to me that He couldn't say in my prayer closet? Well, of course He was going to say what I didn't want to hear.

I dropped everything and left Mike with the kids. I drove to Manuela's and was greeted at the door by my German friend. "Sit down," she said, as she placed a glass of iced tea in front of me on the dining room table.

Manuela sat at the opposite end of the table. As I looked at her, it seemed as though she were pulling an arrow out of her quiver to load and shoot. And shoot she did.

"The Lord said to tell you that you are moving. You are moving away from here, away from Colorado."

The arrow hit me in the heart. He was determined to finish that conversation and have the last word.

I returned home to talk to Mike. I believe the Lord spoke to me first in this situation because I would obviously be the hardest to move. He knew that if He spoke to me directly I would receive and believe, which I did. And Mike was all for it. It bore witness in him. The next question was, "Where are we moving?"

As I prayed about the move that Saturday evening, the Lord told me that we were going to a place known for research. I even had a picture of people wearing white lab coats. This is part of a little game the Lord and I play. He knows I love to read mysteries and watch mystery films. I even developed, wrote, and taught a course on mystery film and literature. So occasionally, the Lord gives me clues when He is directing my steps. He made me and knows my personality. And part of my personality reflects a part of Him. He loves to have fun. In a playful way, He loves to tease me. Since I am His child, and I am made in His image, then my interests and personality also reflect Him.

Excited about Clue #1, I shared the word research with Mike; but we still couldn't solve the mystery of where we were going.

Then an old friend of Mike's called from Ohio. Mike was telling him about his layoff and our impending move. Out of the clear blue, Chris mentioned that a great deal of growth was taking place in Research Triangle Park in North Carolina. Mike hadn't even mentioned Clue #1 to his friend! Was the Lord giving us another lead— Clue #2?

That night we were watching television. A commercial came on for a waste management company. Then in big capital letters across the television screen, we saw: NORTH CAROLINA. Mike and I just stared at each other. My heart was pounding. We knew where we were going. We had the third clue.

Right away, Mike and I started to prepare. Although the older kids were having a tough time preparing for this major change in their lives, our initial excitement was contagious. We were setting sail on an adventure.

But there were other steps that had to be taken, practical steps to get us from point A to point B. One of the things that was in our favor was that much of our life in Colorado Springs was coming to an end. I had already given notice at the college before we knew Mike was going to lose his job and before we knew we were going to move. I had just felt that change was coming. Mike was graduating from college. Brook was graduating from high school. Adam was completing middle school. The house was being sold.

Now, however, there was an emotional factor to consider that threatened to steal my joy and excitement. I loved Colorado Springs. It is a beautiful city sitting at the foot of Pikes Peak. To look at that majestic mountain throughout the day was to see a changing panorama. The mountain never looked the same way twice.

Then there was our church. The church we were attending was a growing church, and we were taught well. And there was such freedom! Although we didn't know the pastor personally, most of the staff at that time had been my students in college, and we cared very much about our relationships with people there.

Leaving our friends was by far the biggest challenge. One day I was lifting weights in the basement. I was burning off some energy when the Lord spoke to me. He said, "Gael, don't suppress your emotions at this time. You need to grieve. As you think about leaving friends and loved ones, just cry. Don't try to hold back."

The tears flowed immediately. I thought about all my students who were graduating. I loved them so much. I thought of the women in my cell group who prayed together weekly. I thought about Tanya, Manuela, and Kim. This was not going to be easy.

I remembered walking around the Broadmoor and camping in Estes Park. I reminisced about meeting Mike at church and marrying him. Our sons had been born in that city. I had years of memories in Colorado Springs and Colorado.

Lying on that bench underneath those weights, the Lord started to remove the heaviness of my heart. As the emotional burdens were removed and continued to be removed in the next few weeks, my focus changed. I started to look forward instead of backward. I didn't want to be like Lot's wife, always looking back. Even though I was sad to leave friends, the pioneering spirit inside me kept saying, "Eastward, Ho."

I prayed, as did my friends, that any soul ties holding us down to Colorado Springs be cut off and broken. I had the picture of a hot air balloon being released from earth to be directed by the wind. The Lord told me that soul ties result when we give our hearts to people, places, and things that are not of Him or in His timing.

We now knew we were going to North Carolina, but we needed to know where in North Carolina. We contacted AAA and ordered materials. Mike went to the library and newsstands to read newspapers and look for jobs. We did our homework. We prepared our resumes and sent them out to prospective employers.

Mike and I both had family on the East Coast who were excited about our move. Mike's family lives in upstate New York, mine live in the Valley Forge area of Pennsylvania, but neither of us knew anyone in North Carolina. We had no contacts. My only knowledge of the state was that it was known for making furniture. That was not a bad feature in my estimation.

As we prepared to move, I realized we were trained and ready to go. Mike and I love the Lord. We had both been through so much in our lives that we trusted God for everything, and we wanted to follow Him. The Scripture that guided us was Exodus 13:21-22 (NLT), "The Lord went ahead of them. He guided them during the day with a pillar of cloud, and he provided light at night with a pillar of fire. This allowed them to travel by day or by night. And the Lord did not remove the pillar of cloud or pillar of fire from its place in front of the people." We were confident that God would show us where He wanted us to settle.

In preparation for this transition, we paid off all but two bills. We had the money to pay everything, but we decided to hold on to as much cash as possible and tried to save money everywhere we could. We had garage sales. We hired a man to drive a private moving van. We received a lower rate by packing and loading ourselves. We even had a moving date, but we still didn't know our exact landing-place in North Carolina.

One day I was reading the AAA book for North Carolina. We needed to find a place to stay until we knew where the Lord wanted us to settle. Since we had already given notice at our house and hadn't received any feedback from employment companies or private firms, we had to take some steps in faith. I was reading the back of the travel guide under motels and restaurants when a town and motel jumped out at me. It was as if the item were highlighted in yellow. My pulse quickened and I found the map. The city was the approximate geographical center of the state and was almost equidistant from Raleigh, Durham, Greensboro, and Fayetteville. I called the motel to ask about their weekly rates. The owner answered the phone and sounded just like my associate pastor. This was too much of a coincidence. The man was so helpful and nice that I could barely contain myself. This motel also had a bonus: it was one of the few that permitted pets. I talked to Mike and we knew where we were going, even if it was temporary. We were traveling to Sanford, North Carolina.

In retrospect, I see elements of Abraham's journey in our own. We left a place where we had opportunities and a "family" of friends. We had to follow God to the unknown. We had to take this faith walk step by step. God only told us what we needed to know when we needed to know it. Avoiding the temptation to look back as Lot's wife and the Israelites had done was essential. Our destination would prove to be better for us because that was where God was taking us. And God made every step of the journey crystal clear for us. We never had to guess at the next phase. Of course, we can see this in retrospect. At the time, the biblical parallels were not always so obvious. But God never left us without a Scripture or peace in our hearts.

We ended up leaving Colorado almost three months after the day that the Lord said events would happen fast. Before we left, several people had prophetic words that we were being sent out as missionaries. As we drove down the highway, I looked over towards the town of Widefield where my dear friend, Kim, lived. "Good-bye, Kim," I whispered as tears clouded my eyes. But the tears were just a quick blur because immediately the joy and excitement took over once again. We were on our way.

CHAPTER SEVEN

This Is Not What I Signed Up For

God's provision is a promise He makes to us. But are we willing to believe Him? Sometimes He has to put us in situations so that we will trust Him. Sometimes He brings us into difficulties to increase our faith and to let us see His power.

Deuteronomy 29:6 (TLB) reads, "The reason he hasn't let you settle down to grow grain for bread or grapes for wine and strong drink is so that you would realize that it is the Lord your God who had been caring for you."

This Scripture became so real to us after we arrived in North Carolina. Of course, we didn't see its relevance until much later. Mike and I believed that our new state was our Promised Land. Because of Mike's education and experience, we believed he would obtain a job quickly making a good living. With my degrees, I could always go back to teaching college, so we weren't concerned about our finances. As we weren't worried about money, we used our cash and credit cards to live.

We arrived at the motel in Sanford that I had found in the AAA book. Six of us stayed in a little suite. Eventually the owners told us about some of their short-term rental properties on a local golf course, so when they were empty we stayed there. The Promised Land was looking better and better. The rental had several bedrooms, a kitchen, living room, dining room, screened porch, and an enclosed courtyard. I had a walk-in closet where I could pray. The walls were painted in my favorite shade of yellow. We were thrilled with God's blessing, provision, and goodness.

Mike, wearing the new clothes we had bought before we left Colorado, started searching for a job. Days slowly turned into weeks and he couldn't find work. We didn't know anyone. We had no friends. But we still had our enthusiasm, and we trusted God.

Every day Mike would comb the area looking for a job. We stayed in prayer and he searched. Meanwhile, we also explored the region and enjoyed our new surroundings. We are blessed with children who trust us, and as a family, we had some of the happiest days of our lives. We played games every night, swam in the pool, and worked out in the fitness center. We never worried about what God was doing. This was our big adventure, and we trusted Him.

But then reality started to puncture our comfortable bubble. As time progressed, the motel had to move us frequently to make room for guests with reservations. Mike became discouraged with the daily and weekly rejections. What was the use of having a college education if he couldn't get a job? We were filling up our credit cards and depleting our cash. Our belongings were in storage outside of Raleigh, and we were living out of suitcases. Emotionally, spiritually, and financially we were pushed to our limits.

Many of our friends and family didn't hear from us because depression caused our family's communication drastically to dwindle. We could only look at each other and wonder if we had made a mistake. I didn't want to be like the Israelites who wanted to go back to Egypt, but I had to wonder where God was in this. Had He brought us this far to forget us? Had we missed Him? Where all the doors had once been open, they were now closed. The holding pattern was endless, and then it grew worse.

We had had such wonderful expectations. We were going to get the dream jobs and perfect house. Hadn't the Lord promised us a house beyond our expectations? Now the hot air balloon had been popped, and we were left stranded. It was so easy to imagine what the Israelites went through in the wilderness. We were in one.

I had just happened to read in the local paper that school had started. The article also mentioned a North Carolina law that if a student missed so many days of school, he or she would automatically be held back the next year. When we checked the calendar, we realized that Adam, our only child in school, was already in danger.

By this time, we had been living like nomads. That particular week we were all once again sharing the small suite at the motel site. With six of us, we felt even more crowded after being in the rental home on the golf course. Peter, who was three years old, sobbed and sobbed as he told us how much he hated that place. His cries broke my heart but also expressed my suppressed feelings. We didn't know what to do.

When we were living in Colorado, I had written a short story about a female journalist who goes underground as a homeless woman. In the story, the woman makes a deal with her editor that she can't tell anyone the truth about her whereabouts. While she is homeless, she becomes sick and is treated by a doctor who takes her in and falls in love with her. But true to her word to her editor, she doesn't tell him the truth and disappears from his life.

As I was writing the story, the Lord spoke to me through it. One night He reminded me of Charles Dickens who would examine the seedy parts of London for material for his books. The Lord put it on my heart to go underground for a day as a homeless person. I once again shared with Mike about God's latest direction, and he didn't hesitate to agree. In fact, he was enthusiastic. We set the date and started to prepare.

We slept in our clothes the night before we became "homeless." The next morning we didn't bathe, brush our teeth, or comb our hair. I wore gloves to cover my manicured hands and wore no makeup—a major sacrifice for me. Mike took out his false tooth (he really got into this) and wore his old military glasses. We dressed as stereotypical homeless people.

Our daughter drove us from our house to a large city park in Colorado Springs. We ducked out of the car and blended into the environment.

As we shuffled along, we saw people staring at us. We walked through sprinklers as a way of cleansing ourselves. As the day wore on, we felt more and more isolated. No one would acknowledge us. No one made eye contact. What had started off as a lark became almost depressing, as we had no other human contact until some men, obvious homosexuals, reached out and said hello. It was not a come-on. It was the only compassion we saw that day. They were as reviled by society as we were. As lunchtime neared and our stomachs growled, we decided to go to a local soup kitchen. At last we would meet some other homeless people and have some companionship for awhile. We were wrong. We were wrong about a lot of things.

No one at the soup kitchen looked like us. Everyone was dressed relatively nice. People were relatively clean. The people there didn't even come near us. When I held my plate out for food, the woman serving me backed away from me. Since the soup kitchen was packed, Mike and I became separated; and I had to stand at a counter between two men. One of the men moved away and muttered some expletives about how filthy and disgusting I was. I lost my appetite.

We finally left. We had listened in on conversations and learned some points about the system in the time we were there. We overheard people talking about where to get clothes. We heard about shelters. A few talked about day jobs. We also learned about the hierarchy of the homeless, and we were definitely at the bottom of the barrel. We probably fit in more with the street people we saw on television. And that is not to say that those people don't exist in real life, but on this particular day we were outcasts.

We left the soup kitchen and followed some of our fellow diners to the main library. Comfortable and warm, we spent some time catching up on our reading there, as did the others. I was in fear of running into someone we knew and only later found out a college classmate of mine was there at the same time.

By now it was late afternoon, and we needed to find a place to sleep. We went to a shelter looking for help. We walked into a place filled with cots and rules. We read over three pages of regulations. I saw people there craving structure and boundaries. Others desperately wanted someone to take care of them. It was so sad. We talked to the monitor who said we would have to prove we were married to be able to stay together. We invented a story on the spot about being rolled and losing our wallets and wedding rings. It scared me that we could lie so easily. We were told we would have to get permission from the police department to stay.

I knew this was out because we knew too many people at the police department. Many had been students of mine. After taking the step to go to the shelter, we then felt released to go home. We walked to a place where Brook could safely pick us up. We were tired and sad. We had seen a side of human nature that was not pretty; it left a lifelong impression on our hearts.

And now we were homeless in North Carolina.

Peter's cries continued to break my heart. I didn't know what to do. Mike and I prayed and asked the Lord for direction. He then put it on our hearts to ask the motel management to let us use their address so that Adam could be enrolled in high school.

The hotel agreed to help us, and the immediate crisis was solved. But we had bigger problems. We had no jobs; we didn't have a permanent place to live. What were we going to do? We couldn't live out of a motel forever.

I went back to the tiny motel bathroom to pray. I cried and cried and cried. All the pent-up worry, frustration, fears, and anger came out to God. I realized that I had been trying to trust Him. I kept trying to put on a happy face when I was around others. I was trying to have unquestionable faith.

In that moment of raw honesty and emotion, God met me. He took the veil from my eyes and showed me what I didn't want to see. The place we were looking for was right in front of us. Our new home was… Sanford.

I was devastated. Now, don't get me wrong, Sanford is a nice little town, but it was not Colorado Springs. We had difficulty with the local accent. We had *thought* we were going to be in one of North Carolina's larger cities. We had *thought* Mike was going to walk in the doors of a corporation and get a nice job. Of course, we had *thought* we would still serve Him as we always had—from the comfort of our own home. We would make money and give to churches, people, and organizations. This was our Promised Land. We wanted to do what we were doing in Colorado but just in a different locale.

When I came clean with the Lord that day in the motel bathroom, I was completely vulnerable and honest. I wasn't pretending anymore. I was scared. I didn't understand what God was doing to us. I knew in my heart that He had not left me, but where was He? As I cried out to Him in pain and in the disappointment of having left beautiful

Colorado Springs for Sanford, North Carolina, He spoke. He said, *"Would you do it for Me?"*

I will never forget the impact of that question or even the inflection of His voice. My cries of pain and disappointment quickly changed to cries of repentance and even remorse. How could I have ever doubted Him? He is my Savior. He has done so much for me. I have never, ever lost sight of that. And now He was asking me to do something for Him. I was so ashamed.

I didn't hesitate to answer Him. I said, "Yes." But then I added, "Please change my heart."

And in that moment, He did. Immediately I was filled with love for my new town and my new state. The Lord then instructed me to get a newspaper and find a house. Within hours we were peeking in the windows of a large, empty house on McIver Street. Within another hour we were filling out the paperwork to rent the house. Everything happened so quickly.

The Lord could have made this easy on us. He could have just led us here. Mike could have walked into a job. We could have found a new house. It could have been so easy. But He wanted to teach us some things first. He had to show us that even though we may be wandering around and not seeing any change, He is still there. He is still moving. We had to be put in a desperate situation so that we would depend on Him. We saw the reality of His provision by crying out to Him and then obeying Him.

He also had to do some necessary housecleaning in my heart. I was not being honest about my feelings. I was not submitting my feelings to Him. I was trying to be cheerful, full of faith, and full of hope. In reality, I was scared.

We also got to see a difference between being "homeless" in God and homeless without Him. And when it was time, God moved. He provided. And it wouldn't be the last time either.

CHAPTER EIGHT

Remember To Read the Fine Print

I went through a major change when God asked me, "Would you do it for Me?" Some might call it a paradigm shift. I guess in my mind I had thought that when Jesus died on the cross for me, that meant I could ask for whatever I wanted, whenever I wanted, and the Father would do it. Kind of like Santa Claus. Of course, I would have to obey the Ten Commandments and lead a relatively obedient life. You know, I would just have to be a good person. Besides, I was hearing everywhere and from everyone all the things that God wanted to do for me. God wanted to prosper me and bless me abundantly, and I was ready for that. I figured I just had to attain a certain level, a certain amount of years as a Christian, and everything would fall into place. Until then I would try to do the best I could until I got rewarded. And I was pursuing God. I knew I loved Him and had a relationship with Him, but it was still all about me. Now I didn't think any of this consciously, but it was there nonetheless. Some areas in my life were out of order.

Obadiah 17 (NKJV) says, "But on mount Zion there shall be *deliverance*, and there shall be *holiness*; the house of Jacob shall *possess* their possessions" (emphasis added). Although this verse refers specifically to deliverance in Zion, there is a divine order presented that is still relevant today.

The first requirement is deliverance. This is the freedom we as Christians experience though salvation. Jesus attained this for us by His death on the cross. Because of His death and resurrection, the Holy Spirit was sent.

Holiness refers to the working of God's character into His people.

They are to be dedicated, set apart, and consecrated. And possessions? Well, in my mind those were the rewards, the personal goodies that an unselfish Jesus died to give me that I was entitled to on this earth. I wasn't thinking of possessing the land or possessing covenant promises, I wanted to possess the material goods.

I had the salvation. I believed in Jesus. And the possessions, well, that was what I was anticipating. But I forgot that holiness part. That was the part I wanted to skip.

When God asked me to do something for Him, my journey was no longer about me anymore. It wasn't about what I wanted. It was about what He wanted. My expectations were being put to a slow, painful death. And this was only the beginning. The cross was now before me in a way I had never experienced before. For the first time, it was about Him and what He wanted.

When we moved to North Carolina, I had visions of sugarplums dancing in my head. After all, God was going to give me a house beyond my expectations. He knew that I wanted lots of windows, a deck, and a porch. He knew what I wanted.

But after living in a motel for a couple of months, we were desperate. We found the house on McIver Street in a market that was short on rental homes, especially large rental homes. As we looked into the windows of this big, old house, we never even noticed the surroundings. We didn't notice the house had electric baseboard heat. It was September and hot. After all, how cold could winter get in the South? We were used to Colorado where it really gets cold.

Then there was the rent. It was only $400 a month. Since we didn't have jobs, this was perfect. We have always lived on a tight budget and have never made much money as a couple. When Mike and I married, the Lord told me that Mike needed to be the head of the household financially. This was necessary for us because of my own fears about finances, and with my education and earning potential, I also had the opportunity to be controlling. The Lord allowed me to work part-time teaching college when I could get contracts, but we learned to live on one income. Whatever I earned paid for outstanding debts or extras. So we were frugal, and the rent on this house was perfect.

The house on McIver Street was about 100 years old. We like living in older homes and don't mind renovating, within reason. After all, we are renting. But we want to be good stewards and witnesses. And wherever we live is home. This house had a wraparound front porch with twelve one-story columns. There were four large bedrooms, two bathrooms without showers, four fireplaces that didn't work, and ten-foot ceilings. Smaller than the bathrooms, the kitchen was an afterthought. It looked as if a utility porch had been closed in to make a kitchen. We were so desperate for a place of our own that it didn't matter.

Although the interior of the house had a fresh coat of paint (dark brown and white), it smelled. The bedroom carpeting was long and shaggy. I am sure bugs lived in those rugs. We just didn't care. Desperate people will hold their noses. What we needed was a home. But once the sense of desperation wore off, our vision returned to normal. And when we could see clearly, we were shocked again by our new situation.

Renting the house was an act of desperation that quickly became a reality check. Moving into the house took a tremendous effort. Because the house had such a bad odor, and because I wanted to know it was cleaned by me, I started scrubbing all the walls. One day I was so tired and sore from washing down walls that I cried out to God to send a friend to help me. Of course, I didn't know anyone, but I really wanted a friend. Within seconds my arm starting moving by itself. It was as if my arm wasn't attached to my body. I instantly knew that it was the Lord helping me. It was my arm, but I felt nothing as the Lord took over the work. A Friend had come to help me. My strength was restored, and I wasn't sore any longer.

As things were put in order, we finally took time to look at our surroundings. What we saw did not make us happy. We were living in one of the worst neighborhoods in the city. The people we saw on the streets scared us. We didn't let the kids play outdoors. I was working in the yard and snakes appeared. I was terrified of snakes! What kind of place had God sent us to that we would live in fear?

One of the first weeks in the new house, our oldest son was asked to join a gang and carry out a drive-by shooting. Then he brought home a young man who used a racial slur to describe the people who had lived in the house before us. Adam stood up to him and said we didn't talk like that. The young man left, and we never saw him again.

Adam asked me later if God had sent us to this neighborhood because we weren't prejudiced. I didn't have an answer, but why had God sent us here? Wasn't this supposed to be our Promised Land? What happened to that "house beyond my expectations" that God had promised me in Colorado Springs? Believe me, this house was beyond my expectations. I would never have expected God to put me in this house in this city. I hated living in fear. I hated smelly old houses. And I really hated snakes.

So once again, I cried out to God and He directed me to Joshua 1:3-5, 9 (NLT). He told me, "I promise you what I promised Moses: 'Wherever you set foot, you will be on land I have given you. No one will be able to stand against you as long as you live. For I will be with you as I was with Moses. I will not fail you or abandon you. I command you—be strong and courageous! Do not be afraid or discouraged. For the Lord your God is with you wherever you go.'"

Uh, oh. No one will be able to stand against me? Be strong and courageous? Do not be afraid or discouraged? I wondered, *What is going on here?*

As I continued to read in Joshua, God gave me a revelation. I had forgotten that battles have to be fought in order to inhabit the Promised Land. I didn't want to fight. I wanted God to give me a nice house, nice income, and a nice life. Period. I would do whatever He wanted as long as those three areas were in order as my foundation or base of operations. So now, not only was I shocked by the realization that I had to live in this neighborhood, I was also shocked to learn my expectations about what God was going to do with us were wrong too. I had taken a little part of what God had given me and had run ahead of Him—again—in my own mind. I had figured out what God was going to do before He did it.

But the Lord, in His kindness, gently reminded me of words that had been spoken over us before we left Colorado. Several prophesies had been delivered about us being missionaries and pioneers. Well, now it was time to live like missionaries and pioneers. And truly, it felt that way.

I repented and submitted myself to God's will. I asked Him for direction on how to fight this battle. But even then, I had not learned my lesson. One night, Mike and I planned to go outside to pray and anoint the homes in our neighborhood as we had been taught as part of our spiritual warfare training. God put us here, we reasoned. We are called as missionaries and pioneers, we thought. We came to take the land, we proclaimed. We were going to take this neighborhood for Jesus, and the sooner we did it then maybe the sooner we could leave. As we started to walk out the door, the Lord stopped us. He said, "If you do what you are planning, you will be killed."

That stopped us cold in our tracks. We closed the door, went back into the living room, and took a seat. Could we do nothing right? Once again, we cried out to God. Even the tools we thought we had didn't work here. The Lord proceeded to teach us about strategy. For now, we were to get our home in order and continue to pray as a family. He would tell us what to do, when to do it, and how to do it. Each city, each battle, each situation requires His tactics and His leadership.

The Lord was slowly putting to death any of our preconceived notions about what He was doing and how He was going to do it. They were His expectations, not ours.

CHAPTER NINE

A Pot of Trust

I have always heard people say that they live by faith, but I didn't know what it meant. Then one day the Lord began to speak to me. I doubted what I was hearing.

Unsure, I asked, "Lord, are you asking me to be part of the faith movement?" I always thought those "faith" people were strange, and I heard how they would "name it and claim it," meaning whatever they wanted they could just believe God for in faith, and God would give it to them.

The Lord replied, "Don't throw out the baby with the bath water."

As I pursued Him on this, the Lord started to show me what it meant to live by faith. He showed me how the faith movement had been misunderstood by some who proclaimed it, interpreted it, or just heard about it like me. When the Lord asked me to live by faith, He was asking me to allow Him to put me in a place of total dependency on Him. He wanted me to trust Him in all things for all things. Freedom that I had never experienced before would be the by-product of this trust. Now, in my brain I did not understand how dependency would bring me freedom, but it was one of the many paradoxes that I saw in this growing relationship with Christ. I just had to trust Him to sort it out later.

I appreciate how the Lord works in that He takes me through transformation step by step. It's not as if I was expected to be like Christ an hour after I became saved. The process of becoming Christlike will continue for the rest of my life. But the degree to which I am willing to trust, believe, submit, and obey will determine the length of the course. In other words, how willing am I to decrease so that He can increase in my life (John 3:30). I understand that if I give more of myself to Him, He will give more of Himself to me. And this is not just about doing good works for Him. This is about me responding to Him in every part of my life—in every part of my heart and in my mind.

To live by faith we have to be put in situations where only God can rescue us, provide for us, and heal us so that we can see how truly great, mighty, awesome, and powerful He is. But too often, we interfere and don't trust God to take us to the end of the process. Instead of letting Him answer our prayers, we get desperate, step in, and figure out a shortcut to ease our immediate pain—only to have to relive the circumstances down the road again. I want to make this clear, that doesn't mean we can't go to doctors or anyone else for help, but we go as He leads us. And this doesn't mean we have to wait for Him to tell us what to make for dinner. But if we can't decide or we do need help, He is there to be part of our lives.

In our society, the cross symbolizes the word faith. At the cross is where Christ meets us and lets us know He has taken care of everything already. We just have to walk it out so that we gain confidence in who He is, in His Word, and in ourselves.

These are not just one-time lessons. We continually have to go through faith building exercises to increase our trust in Him. Several years ago, I was experiencing a particularly demanding time and was crying out to God. Every time I turned to Him, He would tell me to trust Him. When I asked close friends what to do, they would reply, "Trust Him."

Well, I grew sick of that answer. I didn't want to hear the word *trust* ever again. I wanted to know something. I wanted to know what to do. I wanted some action. "Trust" was not the correct answer. That was just too passive.

I went back to the Lord. Once again, He said to trust Him. Exasperated because I was scared in the situation I was facing, I cried out, "Trust! You keep telling me to trust You. I don't even know what that means. What does *trust* mean?"

"I've been waiting for you to ask," He said.

At that moment, I had a vision and the Lord asked me, "What do you see?"

"I see a root-bound plant, Lord," I replied.

Then the vision changed. "Now what do you see?" He asked again.

"Now I see a huge empty pot," I said.

"Child, tell me about a root-bound plant," He said.

"Well, Lord, a root-bound plant will die if it doesn't get repotted into a larger pot. It can't grow." I said.

"Daughter, that root-bound plant that you see is faith. It will die if it's not repotted into a bigger pot. The big pot is trust. For faith to grow it must be placed in a bigger pot of trust. I am causing your faith to grow by placing you in a situation that requires more trust. And when it fills that pot, we'll have to get a bigger pot."

I was humbled. He continued, "You don't have to understand what you are experiencing. If you understood all that was happening to you, it wouldn't be trust. You wouldn't need to trust Me." Later I remembered Proverbs 3:5 (KJV), "Trust in the Lord with all thine heart; and lean not unto thine own understanding." God uses adverse situations to give us understanding. Other times, He just whispers, "Trust Me and don't lean on your own ability to understand."

Time after time, we have been put in bigger pots of trust so that our faith will grow. This is always difficult and scary. When I look back, though, I am always very grateful that I allowed God to move me.

One of the areas that God has chosen to use to increase my faith is in the area of provision. When I was unemployed and single, I saw Him accomplish this over and over again. I learned some of these faith lessons when I was newly saved and still in Colorado Springs. I worked for a company as the Manager of Human Resources and Director of Training. After the company was bought out, the Lord told me that I would lose my job one particular day. Sure enough, the vice-president brought me a pink slip that evening before I left my office. Then my contract wasn't renewed to teach college in the evenings. The squeeze was on, but the Lord assured me that He would provide. During that time, I looked in the refrigerator and noticed we were down to one package of hot dogs. I reminded God of His promise to provide. I closed the refrigerator door and happened to walk to my front porch. The scene that awaited me astounded me. My porch was filled with groceries! The Lord knew my need before I had even prayed (Isa.

65:24).

Another time I gave my last ten dollars to a woman I had met who was in need. She knew I was out of work and asked me what I was going to do. I said, "I'm going to trust God. He will provide." When I returned home that day, $100 in cash was in my mailbox.

And yet another time I invited some women to lunch and fed them what I could. Imagine my surprise when I found $250 under my plate when I cleaned up after they left.

Again and again, the Lord met my needs and increased my faith. Living in North Carolina, however, I now was facing the biggest "pot" or level of trust I had ever faced. He was asking for a lifestyle change, not just a temporary fix of some hardship. He would be glorified through it. Again, I heard His words, "Would you do it for Me?"

I didn't hesitate to answer. Of course, I would do it. But Mike was struggling. One day as he was looking for work and contemplating a move to Virginia, the Lord spoke to him, "Mike, grow where I have planted you."

As the head of the household, Mike was feeling the pressure more than the rest of us. I still had an adventurous spirit about what we were called to do. I took the pursuit of being a pioneer and missionary seriously. We might not be in China, Russia, or Africa, but we were still missionaries. We were on a mission from God.

However, Mike hadn't had the same experiences that I had. He had not seen God move in this area to the extent I had. His faith level wasn't as deep. He had to learn faith lessons on his own. As he was getting ready to look for work one day, he noticed that we didn't have any toilet paper. This was the breaking point for him. He shook his fist at God. "Where are You? Why have You brought us here?" he cried. "We don't even have toilet paper. When are You going to do something?"

As Mike opened the back door to go to the car, he was met by a surprise. The back porch was filled with groceries. In the center of the floor in one of the boxes was a tower of toilet paper. Mike broke down and cried. The Lord then told him that He was bigger than our circumstances, and He would provide regardless of those circumstances. He is bigger than our successes and failures. He is able.

We were out of work for almost ten months. I acquired a job delivering phone books for which I was paid seven cents or ten cents a book depending on the area. Mike would sometimes help me deliver them. Here I was with a master's degree delivering phone books. Then we signed up with various Social Service agencies for help. At times, it was humiliating.

One day we didn't have enough money for even a loaf of bread. I was in the kitchen making bread when I heard a knock at the door. It was the UPS man carrying a large box. I wiped the flour off of my hands, signed for the package, and opened it up, excited as a child. Inside of the box were loaves and loaves of bread! And it was the best bread—sourdough bread from San Francisco! My brother had sent it as a gift, not knowing what we were going through. God did, however, and His timing was perfect!

People would ask us what we were doing to look for work. Only God knew how earnestly we were trying. Every day, week after week, month after month, Mike faced daily rejection. The new clothes we had bought with so much hope and anticipation started to fray. My heart ached for him. Brothers and sisters in the Lord would ask us where the sin was in our lives that kept God from blessing us. At times, I wondered if Job and I had the same friends. During dry times, it seemed that no one supported us. The prevailing attitude seemed to be one that if circumstances were going well, then it must be God. If not, then it must be the Devil. No one understood what we were beginning to see: God was in this. He was purifying us. He was testing us. He was training us. He was raising our level of faith. I asked God about it once. "I don't want to be a charity case," I told Him after another time of receiving food and clothes from someone. We were capable of earning a living.

He said, "Your inability to receive is in direct proportion to your pride." Ouch!

Finally, the week before Mike's unemployment was to run out, he secured a job in Sanford. We were so excited. He was to be part of a start-up team for a company relocating to this area. That same week Brook got a job at Wal-Mart. We were going to have some income!

I could just imagine how much Mike would make as part of this team, especially with his experience and education. This job would really test his skills. We would finally be able to move into one of the nice neighborhoods where our new friends lived. My mind just raced ahead with dreams and plans for the future.

Then Mike came home to give me the news. He would only be making $7.25 an hour working on an assembly line as a technician. I was devastated. What was wrong with us? Weren't we worth more than that? Weren't we the children of the Almighty God?

But God wasn't finished with us yet. He was serious about calling us to a life of faith. Initially we were not happy about it, but over time that changed as we allowed God to work. We began to see that it was necessary for Him to keep us in a place where we would have to be totally dependent on Him. This was not easy on our flesh. The flesh resisted immensely to the pressure. We were literally in a place where we couldn't do anything unless we asked the Lord. Regardless of how big or small, no matter if it was a need or a desire, we had to go to Him. This was part of our training.

One time I wanted to paint the interior of the house. All the dark brown and white colors were getting to me. Since we didn't have the money, I asked the Lord about it. He told me to ask the property manager. So I did. He was sweet and sympathetic, but he informed me that too much had already been put into the house before we moved into it. I let it go, assuming I had heard the Lord wrong.

Three days later, I found a card under the front door. I opened it up to find a blank check inside. The card was from the property manager's father. He wrote, "Steve told me about your request for paint. I see all the hard work you have put into the house. Buy the paint you need."

I was elated! I had heard the Lord after all! I went and bought the paint.

Our first winter in North Carolina was very cold. We turned on the baseboard heat to warm the house, but even then, we could still see our breath in the morning. Then we received the bill: $648.50! Mike had just gotten a job, but we still didn't have the money to pay this bill. What were going to do? We let our church know we had a need, and God did the rest. Once again, confessing our need for help was so humbling. We would rather take care of things ourselves, but that wasn't in the plan.

People brought us money. The church helped too. But major assistance came from an unexpected source. Mike had heard about an agency that might help. As he presented our problem to our contact, a stranger, she looked at him and said, "The Lord has told me to pay the bill." The agency made up the difference except for fifty cents that we paid. He had His people in place, and He came through again. Living by faith gives the Lord so many opportunities to work miracles in our lives if we will just let Him. As an extra benefit, the contact became a dear friend.

As my faith has increased, so has my dependence on God. During the time I became saved, I was a college instructor teaching Humanities courses. As a teacher, I depended on my intellect, and I was also very proud of my academic accomplishments. But the first time I tried to prepare a lecture as a born-again believer, I failed. I wondered what was wrong with my mind. It was gone. I had no mental or intellectual resources. Every time I tried to tap in, I went blank. I still had a memory and could remember facts and figures, but I had lost the ability to process information and put thoughts together. I was frustrated and felt the beginning stages of panic. I had to write that lecture.

Then I prayed. I went to the Source of all knowledge. I confessed my inability to think. I asked God for help. Immediately I started to write, and the lecture came to me easily. The approach was new, but I liked it.

Day after day, this occurred and spread to other parts of my life. Some days I had to ask the Lord to help me pick out my clothes. It seemed that part of my brain was missing, and I had to depend totally on God to make even the smallest decisions. Later the Lord told me, "I gave you your intellect as a gift. Use it as a tool." I had never used my intelligence as a tool. It was my source. And now it was gone. But I also had a new Source. In retrospect it was the best training I could ever have experienced. Yet, at the time, the exercises were very difficult.

As our family grew over the years, more faith building exercises followed, and our lives changed. As I related previously, six days after Mike obtained his real estate license, his job with a local company ended when production moved to Ohio. He was immediately hired, though, by a real estate agency. Now even though he had some severance pay coming, he was not eligible for unemployment because he had signed a contract with the agency. Six weeks later, our oldest daughter who had married and moved away, her husband, Keith, their three sons, and Keith's dad moved in with us. The kids had felt that God was calling them to leave California and move to North Carolina, and we agreed. So our house went from six to twelve occupants in one day. In our house, with temperamental toilets, with only one shower—yes, we can do this!

Keith was a police officer and a hard worker, so we knew he would get work, eventually. But none of us had any income. Twelve people and no income! This was a huge pot of trust.

What the kids didn't know was that the Lord had told us not to charge them rent or to accept any help. We were to pay for the increase in the utilities too. The trust pot was getting bigger. He did say they could help with groceries, but that was it.

Keith's dad stayed with us for a week before he moved into an apartment. For the kids, their root-bound faith had to expand too. Keith looked for work immediately, but it takes months to go through the process of becoming a police officer in North Carolina even with all of his experience. Then Brook found out she was pregnant. Between the two of us, we already had seven children ages two to thirteen living under one roof.

It was six long months before Mike sold his first house, but we had never lived better. Money just poured in from the most unbelievable sources. We were able to take care of all the bills, feed all the people, and do everything that needed to be done. And we all got along too. Keith obtained a job with a nearby police department, and after four and a half months of living with us, the kids were able to move into their own home (Mike's second sale). But as we lived together with no money coming in, we didn't know how long the situation would last. In our hearts and minds, we had to be prepared that it would last as long as God wanted it to—and as long as it took for our new level of faith to occupy the bigger pot of trust.

CHAPTER TEN

Money Doesn't Grow on Trees

God profoundly wants to be a part of every aspect of our lives. Having a personal, intimate relationship with Him makes Him part of our family. He is our Father after all—and our provider. But He is not a Father who is removed and unmoved somewhere far away in His own world. He can be a recognizable active part of our lives in this world if we will let Him.

One of the ways He has shown Himself recognizable, active, and faithful over and over again is in the area of finances. From the very beginning of my walk, He started to speak to me about money. Now this is interesting because I grew up in a traditional church where the minister also used to talk about money. For some reason I remembered those sermons, and they were not always a favorable memory. Of course, that memory came through childlike eyes and may or may not have been true, but it served to form some opinions about the church and money. God had to sort some of this out for me.

When I became saved, I had to trust God for everything; and money was a big part of the trust issue. This was an area that was difficult for both Mike and me. Both of us come from homes where money, or rather lack of money, was an issue. A spirit of poverty hung over us. No matter how much we worked or tried, a hole was in the bucket and whatever poured in poured right out. Each time Mike's job changed, we thought our lives would change financially, but it didn't happen that way.

When Mike and I were married, we had to establish a bank account. I didn't want a joint account. Before I was a Christian, I was married to a man of position who had cancelled all of our joint accounts and credit cards within a twenty-four hour period, leaving me with nothing before he proceeded to divorce me. I didn't want to take that chance again. But the Lord wouldn't hear of it. "Trust me, Gael," He said gently. Then He added, "And put Mike's name first on the account and checks."

I didn't like this at all. I had just a little fear in this area. But I did as I was told.

A few weeks later, confronted by new bills and a small paycheck as a writer for a business newspaper, I was reading the book, *Joshua*, by Joseph Girzone. Inspired and convicted, I cried out to God to simplify my life. He said, "Sell the car."

I couldn't believe what I was hearing. The Lord, my Father, my good Father, was asking me to sell my Audi 5000—my beautiful silver car. Even when I was waiting tables during the divorce process, I was able to keep that car. I was making $2.10 an hour, wearing designer dresses, waiting tables, and driving that car.

But the Lord had spoken. I had to get rid of my car. I couldn't afford either the payments or the insurance anymore. The car payment was more than my rent. And I had asked God to simplify my life, so I felt compelled to do it. Mike was in agreement.

Within one week, the car was gone and paid off. Meanwhile, our friends gave us a car. The car was so rusted out that we could see through it. The cloth part of the roof had been removed. The springs were coming through the seat, or what was left of the seat. Those bobble-head dogs wouldn't be caught dead in this car. My kids were ashamed to be seen in it. They would duck down when we drove by their friends—and we were living in the Historical District of Colorado Springs at this time! One day I was driving an Audi, the next day a Bomb.

Oh, and then there was the parking situation at work. I had a daily pass to park downtown. The parking attendant was there to let me into the lot. Every day I cheerfully spoke to him and waved. The greatest humiliation was that I had to face him now in this beat-up car.

I went to the Lord and asked Him, "Why don't You just pour out all those treasures in heaven on me—abundantly, I might add? Why do I have to be humiliated like this?"

The Lord spoke, "Gael, you pretend to have money, but you don't."

Oh, no. He was right—again. I was pretending. I wasn't being real. My life was a facade, an illusion. My life did not glorify God. This was not good. Did I smell flesh burning?

As part of my job, I had to interview corporate leaders, politicians, and directors of foundations. Now I had to drive to appointments in the Bomb. What would people think? Would they take me seriously? I agonized over the situation.

My next major interview was with the new director of the zoo in Colorado Springs, one of only two mountain zoos in the world. My editor was excited about the story. All I could think of was my car. I drove up that mountain road, curve after curve, muttering about that stupid car. I was dressed for the meeting wearing high heels. Although I had been given permission to drive into the zoo, I chose to park at the main entrance with the visitors and walk up that hill to the director's office in those high heels. My pride hurt my feet. It was one of the worst interviews I had ever done.

But afterwards the Lord spoke to me. He said, "Gael, I was so proud of you. There you were driving up that mountain, complaining the whole time, but you did what I told you to do. You sold that car. You drove the Bomb. The angels and I cheered for you."

Upon hearing those words, I never cared about that car again, and I never cared what anyone else thought about it either. Seeing myself from God's perspective changed my heart. He was proud of me for driving that beat-up, ugly car. God was proud of me! And the plus about that vehicle was that we didn't have any debt attached to it.

After the car incident, every debt was paid off within a few months. My obedience with the car (and my pride) freed the Lord to move in our lives. Money was always tight, but we didn't have any huge debts until we moved to North Carolina. Since we had been out of work for so long, we had used up all of our savings and had reached the maximum limit on our five credit cards as well. We were embarrassed by our situation. How could we have so much debt? How did this happen? We were being so diligent to find good jobs. We were just trying to survive and were very frugal. And we were faithful in our giving regardless of our circumstances.

With the debt, the unexpected low-paying jobs, and the high utility bills, we felt like we were in prison. We were faced with a deeper dependency on God. "Lord," I cried, "We give. We praise. We are thankful. Where is the blessing?"

He said, "Child, blessings are not just those things I give you. Blessings are also the things I keep from you."

Immediately I knew what He meant. I thought of all the bad things that could have happened to us, and I realized how blessed and protected we were. I was thankful. I was blessed.

The Lord encouraged us to keep giving. Once during a particularly challenging time, the Lord told me that we were under siege. He said that the tendency during tough seasons is to horde, but that is the opposite of how His kingdom works. Those are the very times to trust God more and keep giving. And we did. It became our lifestyle.

Sometimes the only thing we had to give was our time. We gave to our children, our friends, whomever. We learned to give whatever we had, and we had to learn to give cheerfully (2 Cor. 9:7) because honestly, it wasn't easy. It was a sacrifice.

One time we didn't have any money to give a friend who was out of work because of cancer treatments. We asked the Lord what we could do, and He told us to give the man some of our antiques, which we did. Our friend was able to sell the antiques and use the money to help support his family.

Another time the Lord told me to empty out our freezer. I separated the food into bags. Then my son, Adam, and some of his teenage friends went out and delivered the food anonymously to different families in and around the neighborhood. The boys were so excited to do their part. But they also knew the sacrifice it meant to our family who trusted God for provision. "What are you going to do for food now?" they asked.

"Trust God," we replied.

We didn't have very long to wait. The very next day a man who had a meat delivery route came to our front door. He said the Lord had put it on his heart to fill our freezer. He gave us more food than we had given away. Then one of the boys who had helped Adam brought us some meat too. God had provided abundantly. What an example this was of sowing and reaping. Mike and I always give out what has been given to us. If we give clothes or blankets away, we always make sure we give items that are in good shape. People are worthy to receive what is good. When food is given, we keep what we need and share the rest. When we are given money, we ask the Lord if it ours to keep or if we are to act as a conduit to get it to someone else.

I remember we were given a huge ham one Christmas. The Lord said it wasn't ours and told us where to take it. When we delivered it, the family told us they had prayed that God would give them a ham. Once we were given $500 in an envelope. We didn't know who gave it to us, but the Lord let us know immediately in our hearts that it was for someone else. That night a friend called crying, needing money to pay her rent. She had specifically called me because she knew she could cry out her frustration without worrying that I might feel obligated to help her in her distress. Little did she know, we were waiting with the money to help her.

We were in church when the pastor asked the congregation if anyone needed money. We thought he was joking. He said someone had found $89 and couldn't find the owner. Several times the pastor asked if anyone needed money. I knew lots of people had needs in the church, but no one responded. Finally, Mike shot up his hand and said, "I need it!"

As Mike walked towards the front of the church to get the money, the Lord whispered to me "conduit." I knew what that meant. When Mike returned to his seat, I told him what the Lord had said. I even told him who I thought should be the proper recipient. Mike prayed for a second and said, "After church, give the money to Joan."

So after church I went directly to our friend and gave her the money. She refused at first, but I wouldn't hear of it. We had to be obedient to God, I said.

Out in the lobby, Joan's husband came up to Mike and said he was glad Mike received the money. Mike just smiled broadly knowing what the man didn't know—that we had just given the money to his wife. Then the man looked at Mike and said, "You know, I found that money on the floor when I came into the building this morning. I couldn't find the owner of it anywhere, so I gave it to the pastor." Mike was stunned. That man's honesty and faithfulness was being rewarded, as well as his need! God had returned the money to him! We laughed all day thinking about what God had done. But the Lord wasn't finished.

Later that same day, the Lord told me to take Peter to a hair salon to get his hair cut. I argued with the Lord about doing something like that on a Sunday because I like keeping that day as a day of rest. The Lord insisted I go.

Peter and I walked into an empty salon, and a woman cut his hair. As I was writing out the check, the Holy Spirit whispered to me, "Give her a tip; she needs the money." I did what I was told and looked up at the woman. I said, "Do you have any prayer requests?"

She said, "Yes, my husband just lost his job, and I am pregnant with our fourth child."

I asked her if I could pray, but before she could answer, I grabbed her hand and started praying out loud. When I was done, she was overwhelmed with emotion. She said, "Everything you prayed was true."

The Lord knew I didn't have the extra money for Peter's haircut or the tip. He knew I didn't like to shop or get haircuts on Sundays. But I was obedient. God wanted to bless that woman who did have to work that day.

So later that evening after being a conduit for $89 and getting a haircut and giving a sizable tip, God blessed us. We received $400 in cash!

Mike and I don't give to get. Years ago a woman gave us a large sum of money and said, "I want a new house, so I am planting this money into your life." Her words disturbed me. She was giving to get something for herself. What kind of giving is that? I didn't like what I was hearing. I believe we should give without any expectations of getting anything in return. I know that I will reap what I sow because that is what Scripture says. Hearing someone manipulate that verse saddened me. God will decide what, when, where, and how I will reap.

At times the spirit of poverty has hung over us. One day while sitting in church, the Holy Spirit whispered to me, "To begin breaking that spirit of poverty, get rid of the stuff you aren't using." My heart started to burn inside. I told Mike what I had to do. When we returned home, we started collecting our stuff. We decided to give everything away to our Hispanic neighbors. It was July, but we said, "Feliz Navidad, Merry Christmas" as we joyfully gave away an area rug, extra computer, dining room set, good clothes, videos, and games. Everything we gave away was nice. We gave the best we had to give, and the neighbors were thrilled. We actually felt cleaner and lighter after we were done.

The next day some friends stopped by with a gift. The Lord had led them to give us their second car! As much as we had given the day before, we could not surpass God!

Many times our giving was a sacrifice. We have given out of our need. One day we were given some much needed food and $20. That night we shared the food with another family and even gave them the money, which we needed very much. We found out later that they had six children, no food, and were $10 short on their mortgage. The next day after praising Him, thanking Him, crying out to the Lord about our own needs, singing a new song, and literally falling asleep while resting in Him, someone came to our door and gave us a check for $250!

Sometimes the Lord requires us to step out in faith. My best friend from Colorado came to visit a few years ago. While she was visiting, the Lord put it on our hearts to go to Washington, D.C., to pray at the Supreme Court. We invited another friend to go with us. The only thing holding me back from the excitement was the money. The Lord had put it on my heart to go, and I wanted to go; but I didn't want to burden my friends. Finally, the Lord spoke to me, "Child, your god is responsibility." He was so right! I had a fear of irresponsibility. Being without money and in debt made me feel irresponsible and ashamed.

The Lord continued, "My children believe more what the enemy says than what I say. Believe what I say, child. When you don't believe what I tell you, it is pride because what you believe is more real, more important than the truth I give to you. Remember that I am not a God who lies. I am not a God of shame. I am a God of conviction. Don't look down at Satan. Look up at Me."

So I put responsibility at the foot of the cross, and I lifted my head up to Him with praise and thanksgiving. It was the beginning of change and a series of breakthroughs for us. That afternoon someone came to the door with money. The woman said the Lord impressed upon her heart to bring us a financial gift. After learning this lesson, God was free to move in my life, and I went to Washington, D.C., with my friends.

When I returned, the Lord put it on my heart to confess my financial sins to a friend. I really thought Mike was the one with the financial sins, but I was wrong—again. As my friend and I started to talk, the Lord just kept showing me areas where I had sinned. I had to repent of heart attitudes about money, money and the church, and about people with money. I had to repent and even make amends to friends I had taken money from as a kid. I wrote letters and sent checks. I had to repent to Mike for not affirming him. The enemy had had an open door into our finances, but it was being closed.

Of course, we were tested. The bank sent us a notice that we had bounced a check. We couldn't understand how that could happen. For once, we actually had some money in the bank. Things started to unravel quickly, and we were in serious trouble. Mike ran to the bank to sort things out and was told that it was our job to find the mistake. We couldn't believe their attitude. We prayed to God for an answer. He said, "Ask your father."

I said, "I am asking my Father."

He said, "I mean ask your earthly father."

I didn't want to do that. I didn't want to go to my parents for help. I have always felt that their money was their money. But we were so desperate, and I believed we had heard the Lord. I had to try.

I called Mom and Dad and immediately started crying, feeling broken. It was bad enough being in trouble, but asking my parents for help was the hardest thing I had ever done.

My parents' reaction was immediate. Dad said, "Don't worry. It is taken care of already." Within hours, money was wired into our checking account.

That day the Lord showed me something about who He is. When my dad said that he would take care of our problem, I saw my heavenly Father at work. When we come to Him with our troubles and fears, He is the One who says, "Don't worry. It is taken care of already."

CHAPTER ELEVEN

Okay, So Maybe Money
Does Grow on Trees

The Lord started to give us direction on how to break free from financial bondage, but this was a process, one that still continues. Specific lessons and strategies were addressed about trust and obedience, sins, mindsets, and pride. Tithing and giving had to be worked into our lives with pure motives until it became a lifestyle. We also had to learn how to praise when we were scared and had nothing because regardless of our circumstances, God is still God.

Financial hardship seemed to run in my family. Both of my parents worked hard at their factory jobs. They never talked much about money, but we knew things were always tight. There never seemed to be enough.

In the fall of 1993, we decided to spend Thanksgiving in Delaware with some relatives. My parents were going to drive down from Pennsylvania to join us. It was the first holiday I had spent with my relatives in many years.

While we were planning the trip, the Lord impressed on me to go to Washington, D.C., on the way back to North Carolina and visit the Holocaust Museum. As we considered this, I saw reports in the newspapers and on the news indicating the difficulty of getting tickets because of the crowds. But the Lord said, "Go."

The night before we were to leave Delaware, my precious aunt took my face in her hands and said, "Your grandmother was from Gyor, Hungary. G-Y-O-R. Two dots over the 'o.' Remember that."

Something about the way she spoke to me made me take notice. She was so intense. Why was she telling me this? What made her tell me this? When anyone had ever asked, we would just say that Grandmom was from Budapest. Now after all these years we find out more specifically that she was from Gyor.

The next day we left for the nation's capital. We arrived at the Holocaust Museum, walked in, purchased tickets, and entered the exhibits immediately, something that has never happened since.

We were walking through the museum and came to a glass bridge. I had just walked over it when the Holy Spirit whispered, "Go back." I walked back and saw what I had missed. On the walls of this bridge were etched cities in which the Jewish population had been annihilated during World War II. Under Hungary was listed the city of Gyor. I was stunned! I sensed a stirring in my spirit. The Holy Spirit was trying to tell me something.

We continued through the museum until we came to a boxcar. Holding my little son, Alex, in my arms, I walked through the boxcar. I couldn't even begin to imagine what other mothers had thought, holding their babies in that same boxcar about fifty years earlier. When I came out on the other side, Mike called to me. Outside the boxcar was a video screen. On the screen were pictures of young Jewish people. The caption read, "The faces of Gyor."

Tears sprang to my eyes. My stomach retched. Emotion welled up inside of me. My head was spinning. Twenty-four hours earlier, I had never even heard of Gyor. Now it was in front of me. What was God trying to tell me?

I went to the Hall of Remembrance and prayed. I heard nothing. We returned to Sanford where I continued to pray for weeks. The Lord never said a word. All I knew was that God was in this.

Growing up we knew that my mother's family came from royalty through my Catholic Hungarian grandmother. It was never a prideful thing, just a matter of fact.

Then on December 20 while I was praying for the salvation of my brother and seeking God about my family from Gyor, the Lord finally spoke. Even though my family came to this country before World War I, they still had soul ties to the land of Gyor, where the atrocities of

World War II had occurred. They had been landowners. They had been royalty. The Lord said, "Your family has a spirit of greed, and they misused my name."

All of a sudden, I saw the spiritual and financial poverty in my family. We were cursed. I fell to my knees and repented for the greed. I repented that my family misused Jesus' name for their own gain. I was mortified that my family had done things I didn't even know about, in the name of Jesus. I was hysterical. I cried out to God, "What about me? I use Your name!"

He replied, "You have been protected and set apart for 'such a time as this.'"

I knew the Scripture reference to Esther 4:14. But what followed was the most intense repentance experience I have ever encountered. The revelation as the Lord took the blinders from my eyes was startling. It was as if one minute I was blind and then I could see, but I was horrified by what I saw. I saw our sin. Water poured from my eyes and nose like a stream. Afterwards I was physically, emotionally, and spiritually exhausted. I felt like I had just been through a battle and surgery all at once. But I recovered.

After the holidays, the Lord moved on me to finish a little story I had written a long time ago. Once I was finished, I was looking for publishing information in the back of an old magazine I had bought at a library sale for a dime. I noticed an ad that someone had circled in red. The ad was for a Christian college in North Carolina. It caught my attention because it offered a Ph.D. in religion. The magazine was very old, but I thought I would least call and see if the college was still in operation. It was.

Deep in my heart, I had always wanted to continue my education, but getting a Ph.D. was a financial impossibility considering our circumstances. But I got the enrollment information and tuition rates. On Mother's Day, the Holy Spirit told me to ask my parents for the money to go back to college. I argued with Him. "I can't do that," I cried. "My parents don't have the money, and besides, it's Mother's Day. I can't hit them up for money on Mother's Day."

The Holy Spirit whispered again, "Do it."

I called Mom to wish her a happy Mother's Day. We chatted for a few minutes before I told her of the opportunity I had to go back to school. Dad got on the other line, and they decided right then to help me. I was stunned. Dad was retired and Mom was still working in a factory. I knew money was tight, yet they were so willing to help. I honestly could not believe it.

Still in shock, I hung up the phone. My parents were going to help me achieve one of my biggest dreams—to acquire a doctorate. But I was concerned about the sacrifice that would be involved. I knew they would give up things to help me. I didn't want that. I went back to the Lord.

"Daddy, my parents will suffer in order to sacrifice for me. I don't want that. I don't want them to hurt," I pleaded.

He replied, "Don't worry. They are going to win a large sum of money, and everything will be okay. I need you to get that Ph.D. for a purpose. Certain people will listen to you because you have that degree. You will lead them to Me."

My faith soared. God had spoken.

We continued to be monetarily strapped. Finances were so tight. One night I was in my room praying about the differences between tithes, offerings, and gifts. I wanted to make sure my heart attitude was right in these areas. As I was praying, I heard the phone ring downstairs. A moment later Brook ran to me saying, "Hurry, it is Grandmom. Something has happened. Run!"

I flew down the stairs, my heart pounding. But I knew nothing was wrong. I just knew something good had happened. I picked up the phone. "Mom?" I said.

"Sit down, Gael," she said. "Nothing is wrong. Everything is right. We just won ONE MILLION DOLLARS! Thank you, Jesus!"

I was floored. I had heard the Lord. He had blessed my parents. Boy, had He blessed my parents!

The Lord reminded me immediately about my prayers and repentance six months earlier. The curse of greed and misusing the Lord's name was broken. The spiritual and financial poverty over my family was broken. God was restoring to my family all that the enemy had stolen and then some. And the blessing for me was that I could go back to college.

Even though the enemy's back was broken in the area of finances, we still had some steps and lessons to learn. Battles were still ahead.

I was in the grocery store one day with very little money in the checkbook when the Lord prompted me to pay for an elderly woman's groceries ahead of me. I told the cashier to ring her stuff up with mine. The woman started dancing in the store praising God. Another time I was at the doctor's office and overheard a young man tell the receptionist he didn't have the money to pay his bill. He told her he would go right home and try to find some. When he left, the Holy Spirit told me to pay it, which I did. Can you imagine the shock when he returned and found it paid! What a surprise for him. And how like the Lord! But for me the Lord stressed the need to keep giving, and give cheerfully no matter how tight finances were. It is a step, rather a leap, of faith to trust God to provide. The widow who gave the mites knew that and was commended for it (Mark 12:41-44, Luke 21:1-4).

Some of my possessions also kept God from blessing us. The Lord showed me that I had some jewelry that needed to be thrown away. I asked Him if I could give the jewelry away or pawn the pieces. The answer was no. I went to the kitchen, stood over the trash can, and recited the words to the song "Lord, You Are," which states that He is more valuable than any possession we could have. I love Him more than I love my possessions. And many times, I had to prove that to the Lord.

Later I asked the Lord why I had to dispose of the jewelry. He told me that the person who had given them to me years ago before I was saved had no legal right in my life. And it was true. The man who gave those pieces to me was not my husband.

Less than a week later, in one single night, people came to our house and each separately blessed us with gifts including a new living room chair, groceries, $400 in cash, a night at a bed and breakfast, and an emerald ring with diamonds!

On New Year's Day several years ago, the Lord put it on my heart to make a list of all our debts. The amount was sizable. Most of it was still credit card debt from moving to North Carolina and being unemployed. We had been carrying that debt for years without making a dent in it. During that time, we received debt counseling in an attempt to find relief without filing for bankruptcy. Every time we considered or prayed about filing for bankruptcy, the Lord always assured us that He would take care of it. So we waited and waited for Him to take care of it.

Eleven months later, I was exasperated by God's lack of movement in this area. I knew the financial curse was broken. My parents were prospering. My oldest children were doing well financially. Mike and I were standing on God's promises. So what was the hold up?

That Sunday we went to a different church. The pastor stood up to speak. He said that the message he had to give was not one usually preached during the holidays, but the Lord told him that if he didn't preach it, he would be disobedient.

I was on the edge of my seat. What was so important that it had to be preached right now? I prepared my heart to be open to what was going to be said.

The pastor shared his story of financial bondage and what God had taught him through it. Then he shared the process God had given him for getting out of debt. But then he said the words that pierced my heart: "Make a commitment to God to use every extra cent to get out of debt, and then see what He will do."

We had never done that! We had an expectation of waiting for God to appear and perform some spectacular miracle (as He had done for my parents). But He wanted something else from us—commitment.

Mike and I made the commitment to God right then and there. Every extra cent would go to relieving our debt. Then the Lord told us to start a savings account right away. We didn't even have the money to put in a savings account! But Mike and I committed to saving $25 a week and then later increased it to $50 a week. Then the Lord told us to go to others who had financial needs. We felt strange doing this because we were in debt ourselves, but we did so out of obedience.

What happened next was nothing short of a miracle. Within four months, our debt was reduced from $28,000 to $3,700! Money started to pour in from various sources. Some of it was expected (like an income tax return), but some of it was not. For example, we owed someone $1000. I called the person and told them I was sending them a check. The person said they honestly couldn't remember ever giving us that money. The key words that the person used were, "That debt is forgotten." So instead, we were able to use that money to pay down something else, and we checked off the debts one by one. Other debts were reduced because we were paying in full, and that saved more money to apply to other debt.

On my birthday that year, I was playfully talking to my heavenly Father and said, "I know You really, really love me. Could you give me something just from You for my birthday? I want a gift from my Daddy."

When the mail came that day, so did almost $11,000! That paid off even more of our debt—a wonderful birthday present from the Lord!

That same summer some friends of ours were visiting from Kentucky. Before we all went to bed, they told us about some land by a lake in a gated community that they owned and wanted to sell for $3000. I couldn't believe it. In my heart, I thought how much I would love to own some land. And I knew this deal was a bargain.

When I woke up, the Lord spoke to me. He said the land was mine. I told my friends I was interested, but we didn't have the money. My friends said they had already discussed the situation and believed the land was ours too. I asked them to give us a chance to see if we could come up with the money. If it was God's will, He would provide.

Again, God provided. Money came to us—enough to pay for the land and the lawyer's fees. We ended up getting the land for free! And someone also gave us a Jon boat, a flat bottomed boat that is perfect for fishing. God had significant purpose in store for that land. New relationships and divine connections came from that miracle. And because of it, the kids have a place to boat and swim every summer too.

So in the course of fourteen months, by following God's strategy for our lives, all our debts were paid off, and we were able to buy some land. And as we prayed for the financial needs of others, what had begun as prayers of obedience quickly became prayers of faith.

But this wasn't the last lesson on finances. More were coming. Several years ago in the middle of this difficult financial time, I had a visitation from the Lord. I was praying one day, and I felt His presence in such a powerful way. Alex, who was three at the time, also knew that the Lord was there. His presence was so powerful that we could almost see Him. Alex sat next to Him on a chair and later played some of his favorite music for Him, dancing around the table. It was awesome. It was also humbling. As we sat together, words can't describe the power of His presence. Words can't describe it because there just aren't any words. I was silent for a time, just basking in being with Him. All I could say was, "I love you; I love you; I love you," over and over again. Nothing else would do.

Eventually He said, "I'm going to give you a vision, and I want you to tell me what you see."

I closed my eyes and immediately I saw two angels carrying a huge treasure chest of money and jewels. Behind those two angels were others. But then a battle started and angels were "picked off" their assignment. The two angels carrying the treasure were slowed down in the process because they weren't covered and protected by the others. I asked the Lord what caused the enemy to come and fight the angels.

"Your doubt," He replied. "Every time you doubt what I have told you, you slow down the blessings coming your way."

I repented for my doubt and unbelief. Later when I shared with my family and a few friends what had happened, they asked me what Jesus looked like. I told them, "When I looked into His face, I didn't see features; I saw love and kindness and gentleness. I saw His character."

The vision about blessings and doubt was just one aspect of His visit, but it did give me insight into His plans to prosper us. Later He gave me a Scripture that took me to a new place with Him in the area of finances and His will. Deuteronomy 8:16-18 (TLB) says, "He fed you with manna in the wilderness (it was a kind of bread unknown before) so that you would become humble and so that your trust in him would grow, and he could do you good. He did it so that you would never feel that it was your power and might that made you wealthy. Always remember that it is the Lord your God who gives you power to become rich, and he does it to fulfill his promise to your ancestors."

I felt that through tests and trials God was preparing us for something more in the area of finances. We had been in the wilderness. He was humbling us. We trusted Him. And now He was preparing us for His power to make us rich and not only to fulfill His promise to our ancestors, but also to fulfill His kingdom purposes. I knew that a transfer of wealth from the wicked to the righteous was coming (Prov. 13:22), but not necessarily for my well-being. It was being transferred for kingdom purposes—to save the very wicked from whom it had originated. This burns in my heart. The wealth God is bringing His people is to be used as He would use it. It is His inheritance. People are being tested and trained for this. We must understand, though, that the money, the wealth, and the treasures are not for us. They are for Him.

After Mike started a new career in real estate, and we went without any income for six months; and after our daughter and her family moved out after living with us for four and a half months, we faced our greatest test yet. Mike received his first commission and the Lord spoke. "Give Me a firstfruits offering," He said. My understanding of firstfruits, which is different from the tithe, is the initial increase of whatever we have produced (Deut. 26). As I pondered what the Lord was saying, He continued, "The firstfruit of nothing is everything."

I understood. This first commission, which we so desperately needed, was in its entirety the firstfruit because we had no income. The firstfruit of nothing is everything. We gave it all away. We never wavered or looked back.

The next two months were the hardest yet. Only one other commission was coming in, and that wasn't even a full commission. And of course, this was during the holidays, which added more stress. Also, we had no insurance and had to depend totally on God to keep us healthy—another new area of trust. So once again, we had to depend on God for everything.

Then the rent was due, and I was praying and asking God for help. Quite honestly, my stomach was in knots thinking about what we were facing. He asked, "Honey, what are you doing?"

"I'm asking You to remember that we have to pay the rent," I replied.

"Sweetheart, what you are actually doing is *hoping* or *wishing* I will pay the rent. You do not believe I will pay the rent. I don't want you to *hope*. I want you to *know* I will take care of you."

My faith went up an entire notch with that word from Him. It was true. I was hoping He would provide. I didn't believe. Something changed inside of me that day. Another lesson from Him waited for me right around the corner.

We couldn't even pay the rent, and I had this crazy desire to go to the local college to receive a facial. They have an aesthetics department there, and the public gets a reduced fee as the students practice. I try to be a good steward. Was this my flesh getting in the way and acting irresponsible? I didn't know what to do. I made a madcap decision and decided on the spur of the moment to go for the facial. This is so out of character for me, but I did it. I was going to spend twelve whole dollars.

I arrived at the college, and the girl was giving me a wonderful facial when I heard the Holy Spirit speak to me, "Give her a good tip." He told me a specific amount.

So there I was, on that table, eyes tightly shut thinking, okay, this "cheap" facial just got a little bit more expensive than I thought. But I purposed in my heart to do what the Lord had told me to do. And as soon as that happened, the woman giving me the facial started to talk about how she had been sick and missed work. I knew she needed the money. I gave a large tip afterwards and told her it wasn't because of what she had shared, but because a loving God had already put it on my heart.

On the way home I just smiled shaking my head, "Lord, Lord, the things You ask me to do." But always the One to have the last word, He countered with this, "Child, because of what you have just done, you will no longer serve money; money will serve you." The release I felt was unbelievable. Spontaneous tears of joy sprang from my eyes. I knew a major breakthrough had occurred.

He continued, "Don't ever say you don't have enough money or you can't afford something—because you can. I know you will use what I give you wisely. You have proven yourself faithful."

Later that year, He told me the same lesson about time. It had become an idol, and I was always saying I didn't have enough time to do things. He said to stop saying that. He had given us enough time in a day to do what needed to be done. He said time, like money, was to serve me—not the other way around. We are not to "serve" time; the very phrase implies bondage and imprisonment.

More tests occurred throughout the year. Over and over, we were taken to the brink of financial disaster only to be pulled out again. Not once did I worry. Then I had a series of dreams where I was taking exams and passing them with excellent grades. I knew we had passed our tests in that area.

But then financial ruin started to creep up on us. Mike's business dried up overnight, and we had no income. "Lord, Lord, what is this? I know the spirit of poverty is off of us. I know we have passed the tests. We believe. What is happening?"

The Lord told me that He was moving us into a new position and using the strategies that we had learned over the years through our tests and trials in the area of finances to get us there. But there was more. He said this wasn't an individual battle this time; it wasn't about us. This time is was for the kingdom. It was a heavenly battle for the transference of wealth. We were part of that battle, and that is why it was so difficult. He said to remember our calling as pioneers and look up what that word means.

The third definition of pioneer in *The American Heritage College Dictionary* is "a soldier who does construction and demolition work in the field to facilitate troop movement." We now understood that the struggle we had faced in this particular area for so long was part of an elaborate godly plan. We were part of a team that God was calling forth to assist in breaking through to advance kingdom finances for His purpose.

CHAPTER TWELVE

Confronting Snakes and Other Fears

For God has not given us the spirit of fear; but of power, and of love, and of a sound mind (2 Tim. 1:7).

One emotion that keeps me from moving forward with God and from hearing Him clearly is fear. It has been said that fear is an acronym for **F**alse **E**vidence **A**ppearing **R**eal. In some areas in my life, I have been gripped with fear, and I have struggled with believing and trusting God. Some of the fear stems from pains or wounds from previous relationships or past experiences. Other times I just battle the fear of the unknown as I move into unfamiliar territory.

When we moved into the house on McIver Street, I was overwhelmed with fear. Darkness seemed to cover the neighborhood. Drugs were sold across the street, and people came to our house looking for drugs. Gangs were prevalent. We were robbed nine times. Our cars were vandalized. A man chased a neighbor with a machete only a few feet from me. Gunshots were a regular occurrence. Murders occurred as well as an abduction. It was not a safe place.

But we knew God had brought us here. We knew it. We knew it beyond the shadow of a doubt. So the question had to be "Why?" As we sought the Lord and His heart, He showed us how much He loved these people. We were not going to be traditional missionaries that moved to other countries. We were a new breed going into places of darkness in our own city and in our own country. And because we were in His will, we would be safer than if we were somewhere that was not in His will and without His protection.

Part of conquering my fear was in confronting it. So my first step was that I had to have His love for the people. Because God had put us here, I then had to use the authority He had given me in dealing with the evil that was present. However, confronting that evil had to be according to His strategy. He would have Mike walk the neighborhood, sometimes alone, sometimes with me, or sometimes with other men. We would just walk the land and pray like Abram (Gen. 13:17).

Then as the Lord led, He would have me bake for neighbors or give them household items. Once He sent us out to ask people if they needed prayer. One group we encountered was drinking alcohol out of paper bags. They put their bags down and held hands in a circle before we could say another word. They had obviously been in a few prayer meetings. Over and over again, He would tell us to respond to Him. Neighbors started getting saved and moving out of the neighborhood. We weren't even the ones to lead them to the Lord, but we saw the changes.

We prayed that God would bring us more people to be saved. We also prayed that if neighbors weren't going to be saved here, to remove them. Some people moved out in the middle of the night. And while we became more comfortable there, we were still careful about allowing people to come into our house or letting the kids play outside unsupervised. We had to use wisdom.

I couldn't help but wonder about the training my children were getting by living in this environment. Family and friends begged us to move, but we couldn't. And slowly a love for our home and neighborhood was stronger than the fear. We still had to take precautions; we couldn't be slack. We knew how to respond when we heard gunshots close to the house. The kids knew to turn off the lights and where to go for cover. It was not the most traditional of upbringings, but necessary.

One evening a man came to our door. He told us he had AIDS and needed money. Although we don't generally give money to people, choosing to meet the need instead, Mike felt we needed to help this man. We brought him into our house and offered to feed him and pray for him. Mike borrowed $20 from our daughter and gave it to the man.

When people heard that we had brought a man with AIDS into our home, they were upset. They said we had threatened the safety of our children. In this case, we weren't afraid. We were listening to God and felt this was His heart in this situation.

A few weeks later, someone knocking at the door awakened us in the middle of the night. We ran to answer. It was the man with AIDS. He apologized for waking us, but went on to tell us that he hadn't slept in weeks. When he had come to our house that day, he had come to rip us off. He said, "I don't have AIDS. I go to churches and target Christians for money that I use to pay for my habit. You are the first real Christians I have ever met. My conscience has bothered me so much that I can't sleep. Please forgive me."

The man repented, and we went on to pray for him. Later we heard he had entered drug rehabilitation and gotten saved. God had His hand on him.

Fear attacked me in other ways. When Alex was born, he had some health problems. Although he was healed, a demon confronted me and told me Alex was going to die. A demon woke me up one night to torment me. Still another attacked me in the bathroom. I kept fighting the fear through prayer, but Alex was having other problems that caused me to doubt. He would stop breathing. He would choke on food easily. Anxiety became part of my life, and I was never at peace.

I was a supply judge for our precinct during an election. Judges are not allowed to leave the premises or get any news. I was on my way to the bathroom when a demon confronted me in the hallway. It told me Alex was going to die. I was in agony as I battled the paralyzing fear that overwhelmed me.

When the election was over, I went home. Alex was fine, but I wasn't. I was plagued by fear. I knew how to take authority over demons, or so I thought, but the demons would always come back. I was so afraid that I was afraid to tell anyone I was afraid. I was afraid that if I told anyone that I was afraid, then something would happen to my son. Logic was totally out of the picture. And the worst part was that I knew it was illogical, but yet I seemed powerless to do anything about it.

Finally, I couldn't stand the pressure anymore. I confessed my fear to my dear friend, Kim, who prayed for me. She prayed for me in faith, and the demon, which had been tormenting me since my son had been born, finally fled. My confession of the fear enabled her to pray fervently and effectively for me. James 5:16 (KJV) says, "Confess your faults one to another, and pray one for another, that ye may be healed. The effectual fervent prayer of a righteous man availeth much."

Kim told me later that as she drove home, the demon then tormented her by saying that because she had prayed for me, her son would now die. But the demon had been exposed for what he was—a liar—and Kim was able to laugh off the accusation. I was never tormented again, and neither was she.

However, other fears also plagued me. I had a fear of being fat. Not obese, not overweight, but fat. After my twins were born, the woman who was once anorexic couldn't lose all the weight. Fear settled in my mind. I was praying in my room at a conference when the Holy Spirit told me that it was my fear of being fat that was keeping me in bondage. While I had other issues to address concerning good eating, good health, and self-image, understanding that fear was as much of a bondage as the thing I feared itself, was a revelation to me. After repenting, I lost almost ten pounds in two weeks.

Other fears also surfaced. I had a fear of getting old and going crazy. I actually had a fear of having too much money, which I feared would take me away from God. The fear of man, fear of confrontation, fear of being misunderstood, and the fear of rejection also plagued me. All of these were strongholds in my life. And God didn't reveal them to me all at once. He gently unveiled them to me over time in different degrees. These fears would cause me to respond to people in unnatural ways. I would shrink back from authority figures, for example, or try to explain myself to people when no explanation was necessary. It was embarrassing.

When Mike was losing his job and becoming a real estate agent, I had some fear about living without a steady paycheck or any insurance. We had thought we were living by faith before on a limited paycheck. Now we had no steady income. So this whole new world of real estate and living totally by faith scared me. But I didn't express it. I'm not sure I was even conscious of it. I just wanted to support my husband and follow God.

Then one night I was awakened by a voice telling me to go to the front. This was not a dream. This was a voice outside of me that woke me up. I bolted upright in bed in semi-fear. I knew the voice was sent from the Lord, and it grabbed my attention.

"Lord, do You want me to pray? I'll pray, but I'm really tired. I'll just lie right back here and start to pray," I said, yawning and falling right back to sleep.

The next thing I heard was the rumbling sound of thunder. KA-POW! I jumped out of that bed and never looked back. I ran to the dining room and looked out of the window to see if there was a storm. But there wasn't. A beautiful moon and stars lit up the night. I then ran into the prayer room and sat in my chair with my back straight and at attention. I was shaking. I knew it was God. And I knew He had something to say. I was silent.

"Daughter, do not fret. This is of Me. Rejoice and praise Me. This is the life I have chosen for you. I will provide and provide well. It is My desire to do this for you."

I remember asking the Lord to help me to praise Him, and He reminded me to make the choice to rejoice. I then started to ask Him for a Scripture, and before the words were out of my mouth, He said, "Jeremiah 29:11." I knew the verse from the King James Version: "For I know the thoughts that I think toward you, saith the Lord, thoughts of peace, and not of evil, to give you an expected end."

Later He instructed me to do a study of the word fret. He showed me that He used that word specifically in Scripture because it is actually broader and deeper than the word worry. According to the *American Heritage College Dictionary*, fret means, "To cause to be uneasy; vex; to gnaw or wear away; erode, to produce a hole or worn spot in, corrode; to form a (passage or channel) by erosion."

Other meanings listed are to be vexed or troubled; worry; to gnaw with the teeth in the manner of a rodent; irritation of mind; and agitation. According to *The Oxford Dictionary of Word Histories*, the word fret comes from an Old English word that means "devour, consume."

My fear about my future was not just some little concern or worry— it was in the fret category. The picture of my body parts eroding or being eaten away was not pretty. Psalm 37 (KJV) starts off with "Fret not," and verses 7 and 8 hit home: "Rest in the Lord, and wait patiently for him: fret not thyself because of him who prospereth in his way, because of the man who bringeth wicked devices to pass. Cease from anger, and forsake wrath: fret not thyself in any wise to do evil."

The bottom line is that fretting only leads to evildoing. Oswald Chambers says in *My Utmost for His Highest* that *fretting* "springs from a determination to get our own way. Our Lord never worried and He was never anxious, because He was not 'out' to realize His own ideas; He was out to realize God's ideas. Fretting is wicked if you are a child of God" (July 4).

The fact that God told me to *fret not* tells me that I was fretting. Just like in the Bible, usually the first words God or angels use to address someone are "Fear not." They used those words because the people that were being addressed *were* in fear. I was fretting. I had gone beyond fear. Fretting is the result of fear that hasn't been conquered.

Fear not only led me to fret, it also led me to be controlling. Fear is the root of control, jealousy, anger, and a few other nasty characteristics. The slippery slope towards "evildoing" had begun, and the lack of peace I was experiencing was due to the fact that I was trying to manage my own circumstances. Control is the fear of losing something.

I went to the Lord and asked Him to help me trust Him. I repented of my fear and fretting. I asked forgiveness for wanting to have my own way, which was to have job security, insurance and benefits. I gave it to Him, and I asked Him to bring His perfect love to those areas where I still was afraid (1 John 4:18). As I cried out to Him, He began to fill me with peace, joy, and hope. It was a nice trade.

Another fear that I had to deal with was a fear of snakes. When I was thirteen years old, I was walking my baby sister in her stroller. We went into a store, and suddenly someone held up a huge snake. I ran all the way home. My mother, of course, wanted to know where my sister was. I had left her in the store! I found out later from a friend who brought my sister home that the snake was a fake.

My apprehension of snakes was so pronounced that I could not look at pictures of snakes or even watch them on television. But it didn't stop there. No matter where I went in Colorado, I would see snakes. One huge milk snake decided to sun itself on my back porch. I couldn't go out of my house until it left. Another one slithered by while I was hiking in the mountains. I didn't even know snakes lived in the mountains! It seemed everywhere I turned snakes appeared. This was getting to be such a problem for me that I didn't want to go anywhere that wasn't a mall. And even there, they would be in the pet stores. To compensate I would walk around practicing my authority by saying, "Die snake, in the name of Jesus!" You just know He has to love me.

I was walking alone in a downtown park in Colorado Springs one day when right in front of me was a very long black snake stretched out across the entire path. I could not go on, but I stood my ground. "Snake! Die in the name of Jesus!" I commanded just as I had practiced. The snake didn't move but didn't die either. I did my command thing a few more times in my most authoritative voice, even changing the tone and pitch. Thank God the snake and I were the only ones on that path.

Finally, the snake moved on, and I continued walking. Not thirty seconds later, I ran into a large German shepherd. German shepherds were next on my list of things that caused me distress! I stood still and quietly prayed until the dog left. I went to the Lord. "What is going on here? I have been confronted by my two greatest fears within a matter of seconds. Why didn't that snake die? Aren't we to have authority over all things?"

The Lord responded, "Child, if you had needed that authority, it would have been there. But you didn't need it."

The fear of snakes followed me to North Carolina. Even though we lived downtown, we had snakes in the yard. Everyone assured me that the various types we had were "good" snakes. Since I was so afraid of snakes, though, I wasn't going to stop and check to see if a snake was harmless or poisonous.

One day I took the boys to a local park when a woman appeared from out of nowhere and said, "We have seen water moccasins sunning themselves by the stream." That was it. I jumped in the car with the kids and drove to Fayetteville, which is forty-five minutes away!

Our babysitter saved our son Alex's life when a baby copperhead went after him. She grabbed Alex and rescued him just in time. That only worsened my fear. That very same day a garden snake spread itself across our driveway. This was getting worse. This revulsion was serious and very real.

Then one day I was asked to speak to a local youth group at a youth retreat at the same place where the water moccasins had been sunning themselves. I hadn't been back to that park since then. I was between the Rock and a hard place. I knew God was in the invitation to speak to these kids, and I had to confront this fear. I was forced to make a choice: walk in the fear of the Lord or the fear of snakes.

I knew in my heart that if God was in this He would protect me. I decided to speak to the youth group and confront my trepidation. However, the night before the retreat, I received a phone call informing me that the location of the event had been changed. The bathrooms in the park were out of order and wouldn't be fixed in time. On one hand, I was disappointed because I had been looking forward to facing my fear. On the other hand, I was trusting God to protect me. He was protecting me by moving the retreat to a safer place.

But the wheels in my mind were turning. If I was willing to go this far in conquering the panic, was I willing to go further? I asked the Lord to free me from this bondage. He reminded me that fear was "False Evidence Appearing Real." I started small. I watched a television documentary on snakes. The kids were surprised that I handled it. After that I progressed to looking at pictures of snakes in a magazine; I had to touch the pictures to turn the pages. But then the big day came when I had to confront the fear up close.

I went to a pet store in town that sold snakes. Inside, ahead of me at the far end of the store, I saw a terrarium with snakes. I inhaled a deep breath, took a step, and said out loud, "I can do all things through Christ who strengthens me" (Philippians 4:13 NKJV). I repeated my actions, and bit by bit, I drew closer and closer. Sweat formed on my upper lip, but my fear of God was greater than my fear of snakes. A knot started to form in my stomach, but I wouldn't quit. I got closer. I could see the snakes clearly now, wrapped around branches in the tank. I took another step saying again, "I can do all things through Christ who strengthens me." I could actually see the snake looking at me now. It was watching and waiting. We were almost eye to eye. It didn't move. I could even see its teeth. I took one more step. "I can do ALL things through CHRIST who STRENGTHENS me," I said one last time. I was now face to face with my fear. And it was RUBBER! It was a rubber snake! It was a fake. I remembered what the Lord had reminded me. Fear is false evidence appearing real. I was free!

A few weeks later, I was at my friend's house. In a jar on the front step was a baby snake. Her son wanted me to look at it. I started to back off but remembered that I was free and fearless. I picked up the jar and looked inside. I didn't like what I saw. The Lord said, "I didn't say you had to like snakes; just don't fear them." I was healed.

I still don't like snakes. But the fear of them is not going to rule my life anymore, and I don't see as many as I used to either.

CHAPTER THIRTEEN

Talent Is NOT on "Loan" From God

Genesis 1:1 (KJV) says, "In the beginning God created the heaven and the earth." The creation process continued and verse 27 says, God "created man in His own image, in the image and likeness of God He created him: male and female He created them." What we learn first about God is that He is the Creator. Then we learn that we are made in His image. So if we are made in our Father's image, and He is the Creator, then we are creators too. Our creativity may come in different areas or forms, but we all have the potential to create.

I was teaching art appreciation at a Christian university when I developed exercises to prove my point. Within two weeks my students, who were just trying to fulfill a humanities requirement, were painting, drawing, and creating. They did this without any art lessons. Watching them catch the vision was exciting.

One night the Lord spoke to my heart while I was praying. He said, "What is one thing you really dislike in life?"

"Oh, that's easy, Lord. I can't stand hypocrisy," I replied.

"Then why aren't you practicing what you're preaching in your art appreciation class?"

I knew He was right. I was teaching something that wasn't part of my own life. I believed everything I was telling my students with all of my heart, but I wasn't living it. As part of my art history studies, I had taken a couple of art classes, but I was definitely not an artist.

I went to my students and repented, telling them I was a hypocrite. I required something of them that I did not demand of myself. And I learned another lesson too. Many of us believe what Scripture says, but we don't do it. We don't live it. We stand up and preach it, teach it, and speak it; but we don't do it. That's what I had done as a teacher, and I was wrong.

I kept myself open to trying different artistic mediums, but nothing clicked. I was willing, though, to let God direct me. I never had any desire to be an artist. It never even crossed my mind. My undergraduate degree was in English with minors in art history and humanities. My master's degree was in humanities with an emphasis in dramatic literature, art history, and music history. My doctorate was in religion. Everything I did was purely academic, not creative.

After we moved to North Carolina, unpacked the boxes, and had everything in place, I was talking to the Lord about one of the bedrooms. I observed, "Lord, this room needs something to bring it together. What do You think?"

"It needs a border," He replied.

"That's it! You're right! But I can't afford the cost of the type and length of border this room would need."

"But you can afford to hand paint the border yourself," He said.

With that He gave me a vision of how I could simply paint a border two feet down from the nine-foot ceilings. Mike drew in the lines for me, and with the Lord's guidance and a tall ladder, I did it. It wasn't perfect. It certainly wasn't professional, but I had done it.

Then at church I was asked to paint Thanksgiving centerpieces. I didn't want to do it. I was so scared; I just didn't know what I was doing. No one seemed to hear me when I tried to communicate that this was not my thing. But the Lord told me to do it and said He would help. So I painted wooden turkeys.

The Lord started to expand my skills in the area of decorating too. I painted the dining room, but the color I chose was too bright and looked horrible. I took the paint back to the store and asked them to tone it down. I painted the room again, and it still looked bad. This was becoming an expensive mistake. I cried out to God for help. He said, "Praise Me."

I was doing this project in the middle of the night, but it didn't matter. I stood in the center of the dining room and started to praise God. Then the Lord told me what to do. He said, "Take some white paint and add water. Then take a rag and wipe it over the dry paint."

I did as I was instructed. The result was beautiful! The bright paint was toned down and had a slightly pickled effect. I loved it! Then I painted a flower garden as a border around the room. That room became our "Joy" room.

I continued to allow God to work in my life in this area, little by little. As the Lord encouraged me to expand creatively in different areas, I often felt insecure. My confidence was low. The word confidence comes from Latin, meaning "with faith." When my confidence was low, so was my faith. I very rarely liked anything I created. As a person who had studied the best in the arts, I knew what was good. And nothing I did was good. But I had to start seeing the works of my hands through God's eyes.

One day He gave me a Scripture that I had not seen before. The verse was Isaiah 45:3 (AMP): "And I will give you the treasures of darkness and hidden riches of secret places, that you may know that it is I, the Lord, the God of Israel, Who calls you by your name."

The Lord told me there were things inside of me that He had never revealed to me before. I had no inkling they were even inside of me. I had to trust Him to expose them. They would be surprises.

At the beginning of every year, I spend time alone with the Lord and seek Him for a word for our family. Every year He meets me. A few years ago, He told me that that particular year would be the year of "breakout" for our family and to look up the meaning of that word. The American Heritage College Dictionary defines a breakout as "a forceful emergence from a restrictive condition or situation."

Okay, so in all honesty, when He first gave me the word breakout, I instantly thought of my skin erupting with little red pimples. Then I thought of a prison breakout. I was uncertain about where He was going with this word.

Then He spoke, "Honey, it is not a bad thing that I am doing in you. It is a good thing. It will shake you up, but it will be good and exciting. You will see Me work a miracle in your life—a miracle—and I will be glorified as you have asked. There will be no doubt that I am a great big God."

At that moment, He gave me a vision and continued. "I have given you a vision of a butterfly breaking out of its cocoon. What a miracle that is! What beauty! And then the butterfly flies. It does something it has never done before. It does something it hasn't even been trained to do. It soars. And so will you. The preparation was in the growth and the perseverance of growth through life. But then the butterfly flies and it is a miracle.

"Keep in mind the picture of the butterfly breaking out because that is the beauty of what is going to happen to you and your family. Just believe. And do not—and I repeat—do not be afraid. Honey, it will be exciting. It will be nothing to fear. So do not be afraid."

Two months before this happened, I happened to meet a man named Allen Montague who was displaying his paintings in Raleigh. As I looked at them, my heart beat faster and excitement bubbled up inside of me. He told me how he painted without brushes. He painted with his fingers. The little girl inside of me responded with delight: *I want to do this too!* A month after the Lord spoke to me about the butterfly, Allen became my teacher. I learned what I never had the chance to learn as a child, and I became a finger painter. I was doing something I had never really done before. The butterfly was free.

Finger painting requires a childlike heart. There is no perfection; mistakes are forgivable. There is no control; freedom is encouraged. It's messy; it's fun; and it's beautiful.

But finger painting means even more to me. It's worship. When I paint, it is for my heavenly Father, the Ultimate Artist, and the Creator of all things. I come to Him in the simplicity of childlike faith and joy, expressed in the simplest of artistic forms.

The Lord has taught me so much about who He is through my paintings. When I paint, I sense in a very tiny way how He feels about His creation. First of all, I love what I do. I put every part of me into my work. Sometimes the imperfections of a painting add interest just as our imperfections do. Sometimes I paint scenes that make me think of places that only God sees, like flowers that bloom in regions that no human being has ever seen, but were placed there for God's pleasure alone.

The Lord spoke to my heart through Ephesians 2:10 (NLT), "For we are God's masterpiece. He has created us anew in Christ Jesus, so that we can do the good things he planned for us long ago."

God looks at each one of us as His masterpiece. His heart is to see each person find his or her unique gifts and individual purpose through relationship with Jesus Christ. As the Lord told me, "I want you to be yourself so I can be Myself." God wants to express elements of Himself through us. And He has given all of us a gift of that expression. My expression comes out through the arts and through my ability to communicate. Some people serve or have gifts of mercy or finance. We all have something unique to us that is from Him.

At first I thought God's only purpose in my art was for me to worship Him and for Him to entertain me. I love painting! But then one day He told me to go to a restaurant in town at a certain time and make an appointment with the owner. I did as I was told. I said what He told me to say. I even wore what He told me to wear. The owner made the appointment for the following week.

I went back to meet with her, taking my paintings with me. Her response was immediate. She wanted to show them in her establishment. When I told her they were finger paintings, she couldn't believe it. No one could.

I showed my paintings for two months, and new doors opened up to me as a result. I was invited to join an art club and many more opportunities arrived. I met new people, had more shows, and started to grow as an artist.

Being an artist also brought problems. My dilemma was that I was painting for God, but my work was being seen and judged by people. The first year I was in a judged show, I was critiqued by other artists. For months afterwards, I agonized over my paintings, finding no peace in what I was doing. I finally realized that I wasn't painting for the Lord anymore; I was painting for other artists. I wanted their approval. This proved to be a very painful lesson. I had to let go of what they thought and only seek God's approval. I needed to learn from them but not paint for them.

I started to see a greater purpose in what I was doing. Just as He had desired me to obtain my doctorate to touch others, now I saw that my artwork was opening doors to an unsaved group of people. My heart started to connect with other artists who became my friends, and I loved them. There was purpose in painting!

It wasn't just through art that the Lord showed me what I could do through Him. One time I was praying intensely. It was one of those times where I said, "Oh Lord, I'll do anything You ask of me." By now I should be smart enough not to pray that kind of prayer. However, when the Holy Spirit puts that kind of prayer on my heart, I just have to blurt it out or I will burst inside.

No sooner had I prayed than the Lord said, "I want you to sing for Me."

I started to sing. Then I realized He had more in mind for than just singing to Him from my bathroom, which doubles on most days as my prayer closet. When I tell you I am not a good singer, I am sincere. But I responded in faith, "Lord, You provide the opportunity, and I will sing for You."

Within days, the president of the women's ministry at church asked me to sing. "Are you crazy?" I asked.

Then I remembered what I had prayed and what the Lord had told me. I looked at this woman with my teeth clenched and accepted.

The next few weeks were miserable for me. A friend played the guitar and rehearsed with me. But the songs didn't sound like me. The day before my debut, I went to the Lord.

"I can't do this. This music is not me. I don't have a lyrical voice. Why did You ask me to do this?"

After I was done whining, He asked, "What would you like to sing?"

"I like Broadway musicals. You know that."

"Okay, then why don't you sing 'My First Love Song' from *Roar of the Greasepaint, Smell of the Crowd*," He countered.

The following night I sang. It was horrible. I ran out of the church as soon as I could. I wanted to die. How could I be so stupid as to sing a song from a Broadway musical and a cappella at that. Our church was known for its singers. I could be a real embarrassment to their reputation.

I went home to pray immediately. I was embarrassed and ashamed to face my Father. My face was red; my head hung down. I desperately needed to cry, but the tears wouldn't come.

"Well, I did it," I said.

"I know. And I am so proud of you. Thank you, child—for singing for Me," the Lord said.

"Are you kidding me? I was awful. No one liked it. No one said a word. Everyone was embarrassed for me."

Very gently He spoke. "Who were you doing it for? Them or me? I thought it was beautiful. I know what you went through to do it for Me too. Thank you, child."

I finally cried—not because I was embarrassed or ashamed, but because He loved me so much. It could have been a handful of dandelions that I brought Him, but it was the most beautiful thing in the world to my Daddy.

Several years ago, I was asked to sing for Women's Aglow. Once again, I became anxious about having to do something that I was not good at in front of people. "Lord, if You are going to ask me to do something like this, at least let me do it well."

I found a song I could sing passably and prepared. Then I partially lost my voice. I was mortified, but I knew in my heart that I couldn't cancel this event. I had to sing regardless of how badly I sounded. Before I sang, I shared with the audience in a very rough voice what I was experiencing. I told them I cared more about what God thought than what they thought. I then challenged them to ask the Lord what He wanted them to do for Him and challenged them to find a gift they could give Him.

Once again, I felt like I was a little child giving my Daddy a handful of weeds. I thought of all the gifts my children had made for me over the years. I remembered past Mother's Days eating burnt toast and ice cream mixed with milk for breakfast. My kids' eyes were shining, waiting to see my reaction. That is what God wanted from me. He wanted that burnt toast made just for Him because I loved Him and was doing the best I could. He is not as interested in our perfection as He is with our hearts. First Samuel 16:7 (NIV) says, "The Lord does not look at the things man looks at. Man looks at the outward appearance, but the Lord looks at the heart."

Afterwards I had such peace. I knew I had done it for Him, and I didn't care what anyone else thought. I didn't look for affirmation from anyone that night. But later a woman came up to me and said, "I heard what you said. The Lord has been asking me to dance for Him for some time. Because of my weight, I don't do it because of how I will look. But I will now."

I knew the Lord was pleased. A week later the same woman called to tell me that she had danced at church, and the Lord moved mightily that day because she had been obedient. God is waiting on us.

A week later, I was contacted by a Hispanic church to put together a praise and worship team for a citywide event. I went to the Lord and asked Him what I should do. "Do it," He said. I was being stretched again.

As I sought the Lord with all of my insecurity and doubt, He gave me some points to consider. He said, "Gael, I can find skilled musicians and talented singers anywhere, but what I want are people who will worship Me from their hearts. That is why I chose you to do this. I am not as interested in the quality, skill, or sound of the voice as I am in the condition of the heart—a heart turned towards Me." I was humbled again.

It wasn't just through the fine arts that God taught us about creativity. Mike and I felt strongly that everything about our lives should glorify Him and bring Him honor. Over the years, people criticized us for spending money to repair the homes we rented. They thought we were wasting the little money we had by investing money in the houses that belonged to others. Granted, I enjoy a certain standard of living. The bottom line for me is this: how I live is a reflection of God in my life. That is not to say that I spend all my time fussing over my house, but it is important to me. What is more important to God is the condition of my heart, not my house. When one is in order, the other follows.

When we moved to North Carolina, both Mike and I found new talents that we didn't know we had. If we had had money, it would have been too easy to go out and buy things or pay someone else to do the work. By not having a lot of financial resources, we not only had to depend on God, but we found out what was inside of us. Mike has always been handy, but now he had to learn how to do even more. His hidden talents were forced to the surface. Our house had no shower, so he furnished one. He installed windows. He fixed toilets. He repaired broken furniture.

As people saw what we were doing, they "encouraged" us by bringing us furniture and appliances they didn't want anymore.

Personally, I didn't like being treated as if we were a drop-off site for junk. One day some friends gave us an old entertainment center that looked like it was from the sixties. It just wasn't our style. It was dark and ugly. Mike and I just stared at it. What in the world were we going to do with this monstrosity? Where were we going to put it? I prayed. James 1:5 (TLB) says, "If you need wisdom—if you want to know what God wants you to do—ask Him, and He will gladly tell you. He will not resent your asking."

I know God cares about every aspect of my life, and He wants to be included in each area. It makes Him more a part of the life of my family and me.

So as I prayed, God gave me an idea. He told me to have Mike cut the monstrosity in half and even out the shelves to make two matching bookcases. We used molding around the edges to dress it up and finished the project by staining the halves a mahogany color. The bookcases are beautiful. We found a nook for them, added chairs, and now have a restful place where Mike and I sit, read, and talk when he comes home from work.

We were also given a drop-leaf table with chairs. This was an answer to prayer because we needed a bigger table for our growing family. It was so ugly and damaged, though, and I was tired of having to fix everything that came into our house. One day I was whining about the work that it would take to fix this piece of furniture. The Lord said, "I want to teach you something through this table."

Mike decided to paint the bottom of the table hunter green; he then sanded and finished the top by painting it white. It took some work, but when we were done it was beautiful. Then the Lord spoke to me, saying, "When I took you into My family, you were unfinished and damaged too. I sanded and smoothed over your rough spots as Mike did to this table. I filled in the holes and the gaps. I do all of this lovingly and with great care. When it is finished, you are beautiful and functional."

That table meant so much to me after I saw it through God's eyes. I saw myself in that table. God had accepted me the way I was and made me into something He could use.

The Lord set this in motion to remind me of an incident that had happened when we still lived in Colorado Springs. I was living in a house that had a fireplace surrounded by the unique Van Briggle tiles. Day after day I would scrub that fireplace trying to clean it. Every time I looked at, it I could see it the way it must have looked originally— shining and bright. Regardless of my efforts, it still looked dirty. In my eyes, though, I always saw it as it was supposed to look. It was always beautiful and clean.

One day the Lord spoke to me. He said, "You know how you see that fireplace? It's always shiny and bright to you. Well, that is how I see you. No matter how dirty you might be, I see you the way you are going to be—the way you were intended to be." What a beautiful picture of how God sees us!

As we continued to press in and depend on God for everything, we saw our talents grow. Every piece of furniture in our house has a story. We found we had talents we didn't even know we possessed—those treasures hidden in darkness. We also saw our confidence in what we could do through Christ grow as well. Our faith was deepening.

God's creativity is without limit. When I needed to do something for my parents' fiftieth wedding anniversary, I went to the Source of all creativity. Since Mom and Dad lived in Pennsylvania, I needed to do something special that could be coordinated from North Carolina. Money was also very tight, so I asked the Lord for help. He gave me a wonderful idea. He told me to have gifts delivered to Mom and Dad hourly throughout the day of their anniversary. He told me to write to friends and family explaining what we were doing and ask if they would like to participate. The response was enthusiastic. People signed up for different hours or sent money. Not only that, unbeknownst to Mom and Dad, we had articles printed in the local papers along with their pictures.

So starting at nine o'clock a.m. on their anniversary, gifts started arriving at the door every hour. Flowers arrived. Balloons appeared. Candy was dropped off at their home. Pizza was delivered at noon. After several hours, my parents recognized the pattern and started to anticipate what would happen next. The last gift to be delivered was a calendar made especially for them chronicling their lives.

Expecting to be picked up by friends to go to dinner that evening, they were surprised to find a limousine waiting for them. The chauffeur drove them to their favorite restaurant where they were ushered into a back room and amazed again. Family from North Carolina and Delaware was there along with my parents' friends. One of the highlights of the evening was a three-tiered anniversary cake. We learned that Mom and Dad had never had a wedding cake when they were married. God had thought of everything!

Of all the areas of creativity that God was uncovering, one area in my life wasn't hidden, but it wasn't used either. I played the flute and piano. I was never a very good pianist even though I had an old baby grand piano. I wasn't worthy of that beautiful instrument. When I took lessons as a little girl, I was taught to play only for my own enjoyment because my hands were so small. I accepted that decision for my life, but in my heart was a full orchestra. Where I didn't have technical ability, I had passion. Several times I tried to play in public but nerves got the best of me, and I couldn't play without making mistake after mistake. I accepted the fact that I wasn't any good and played just for me.

The flute was different. I played that instrument well, and I participated in concert and marching bands starting in fourth grade. But as I grew older, I very rarely played.

Then I went to a church with a worship team that was looking for musicians. The Lord started dealing with me about playing the flute, but I didn't want to do it. Too many years had gone by, and my mouth and fingers were out of shape.

One day someone on the team approached me and asked me to join. I knew it was God since He had already been dealing with me about this. With tears in my eyes, I said yes.

For several years, I played the flute and rhythm instruments as part of the worship team. I also performed at a few weddings. Then the Lord asked me to play guitar, and I just picked it up and started to play. I wasn't good, but I was enthusiastic. The word enthusiastic comes from the Greek *enthousiasmos*, which means "to be in God or inspired by a god." Well, God inspired me! I was excited by all the new things God was doing in me and through me.

Always in the back of my mind, though, was my inability to play the piano. And then one day the Lord addressed it. He started off by having me break the curse spoken over me when I was little which, in essence, implied that I would never amount to much as a pianist. First, I forgave my teacher. Then I accepted what God had said about me, which was that I could play. Lastly, He gave me a strategy for improvement. He told me to play for a dear friend who would sit with me and without judging would let me make mistakes. Laura had offered to do this for me before when she realized I had a fear of playing in public, but I hadn't taken her seriously. Now I knew this wasn't an option for me.

Laura started coming to the house, and I played for her. She would just sit and listen like a patient piano teacher with a bad pupil. This went on over time.

Then one day the Lord told me to step down from the worship team. I was stunned. I loved playing with them. We had a great leader who was a true worshiper, and there was such unity on the team. I was overwhelmed with sadness at the thought of not being part of the team. But then the Lord told me He had a plan. He wanted me to play on the children's worship team that played at the same time as the main worship team. At this thought, the darkness in my heart was exposed.

In our growing church, many people may not have known my name, but they knew who I was. I was the flute player. If I played for the kids, no one would know me. I could feel the Lord's eyes on me as this was brought to light, and since He already knew what was in my dirty little heart, I didn't hold anything back.

"Well, Lord, you know what I am thinking. I won't be seen. No one is going to know me. Help me."

I repented. Before I was through, a new excitement rose up inside of me.

Then the Lord said, "You are going to experience a miracle."

I wondered what that was about, but I didn't have long to wait; I found out the very next day. I sat down to play the keyboard when all of a sudden I could read chords. One of the reasons I was challenged musically on the piano and keyboard was that I could read music, but I couldn't play chords. I felt that as a musician I was inferior because as much as I tried, I couldn't comprehend chords. Of course, playing the flute I didn't need to know how to read chords.

Now, the day after obeying my Daddy, I could read chords! All of a sudden, after playing piano since I was in second grade, I could read, understand, and play chords. It was a miracle! But God wasn't done.

I joined the little band in children's church. Three other musicians were on the team. Two of them didn't have very much experience. I was able to sing, play flute, keyboard, guitar, and rhythm. Then I wrote some music too. It was too exciting!

Later, Mike and I were released from our church to help plant a new one. I was asked to play keyboard for the new worship team. As I played the first song before our little congregation, I had a vision flashing back through all of the steps that had been taken to get me to this moment in my life. I saw myself as a little girl practicing; I saw Laura sitting with me patiently; I saw the worship team I had played with for years; and then I saw the children's team where I had played for Him. Then I heard the Lord say, "Don't despise small beginnings."

I knew what He meant. I knew the Scripture in Zechariah 4:10 (TLB). All those small steps I had taken were actually leading somewhere. The faith, the trust, the obedience, the lessons, the practice—everything had purpose in a much bigger plan, and only He knew where it was going.

God made something else clear to me through the parable of the talents (Matt. 25:14-30). Although the word talent in the story refers to money, the story is about using whatever gifts or abilities that are given to you. We are not called to hide our talents. We enter into the joy of our Creator when we use them and invest them for Him. To those who use their gifts, more will be given. Those who don't use their talents or gifts will lose whatever they have been given.

CHAPTER FOURTEEN

Cinderella, Dr. Jekyll and Mr. Hyde, and Other Stories

I was walking down the stairs one evening when the Lord spoke to me. He asked, "Would you like to be with Me in heaven tonight?" The question threw me. I wasn't sure if it was a rhetorical question or if He was asking me if I was ready to die. But I didn't think that He was asking me to take a temporary trip.

Always being my honest self, I paused on the steps and said, "Calgon, take me away."

The Lord said, "I don't want you to think of heaven as a place where you can escape this earth. I want you to want to go to heaven to be with Me because you love Me."

I froze. What He was saying to me was so profound. And I knew my heart was not right, nor was it ready to receive Him as my Bridegroom. I had never considered going to heaven to be with my Savior because I love Him or because I was in love with Him. I always considered heaven to be a place where I would pass on to after I died. And so began a journey of love between the two of us.

The Lord began to reveal more to me: "The church is My Bride. And it is being prepared for Me. I want My Bride to love Me for who I am. I want My Bride to be in love with Me. And I want My Bride to reflect our love in their marriages on earth. That is a witness to the world of My great love."

I knew my marriage to Mike did not reflect that love. When we were married, we both brought a lot of baggage into our relationship.

We were both hurting people, but we were hurting people who loved each other as much as we were able to at the time. And we knew we were in God's will.

I particularly had difficulty receiving love. I was afraid of making another mistake. I was afraid of my own poor judgment when it came to men, and I was afraid of being hurt. In a sense, I was afraid of men. And although I had a wonderful relationship with the heavenly Father, Jesus as a man was harder for me to understand or accept.

When I first became saved, I heard a preacher say that Jesus was looking for His Bride. I was so innocent that in my mind I raised my hand and volunteered to be His Bride. In the traditional church I never heard of this concept of the bride and bridegroom before (John 3:29; Eph. 5:25-27; Rev.21: 9). I can just imagine the Lord smiling at me, volunteering to be His Bride.

The statistics for divorce in the church are staggering. I have read some reports that put it at fifty percent, which is at least as high as secular society if not higher. A very real enemy is at work still trying to come between man and woman just like in the garden of Eden. He wants to destroy the sanctity of marriage because it reflects the marriage of Jesus and His Bride, the Church, which is important to God.

When the Lord questioned me that night on the stairs, He was putting His finger on a very serious issue not only in the Church, but also in my own life. I thank Him for being so kind to me.

I submitted and allowed the Lord to teach me about His love and specifically as it related to marriage. First, I had to let Him show me how He saw me. He gave me a vision of a peasant girl in a crowd going to market. She is nothing special in her own eyes and blends into a throng. Then all of a sudden, a handsome King rides into the market-place on a white horse. He sees her in the crowd and their eyes meet. The girl knows at once that He has been looking for her and that He loves her. His eyes see straight into her heart, and even though she's not perfect, He loves her anyway.

The vision pierced me. I knew I was that peasant girl, and the King was Jesus. Jesus loved me and had chosen me. He showed me another vision of a Captain choosing teams, and I was chosen to be on His team. I wasn't picked last like in school because I was a girl and small.

He chose me because I was good and had something worthwhile and of value to contribute. I was chosen because He wanted me. I was part of His team.

Then one day the Lord showed me my heart. It was made of ice. He said I had a virgin heart that had not been given to anyone, and I knew it was true. I was an ice princess. My heart was like an iceberg, so I asked Him to melt it. He said He couldn't do it too quickly because it would be too painful. In the vision, I saw Him pull out a blow dryer and slowly start to melt my heart. But this took time, and I had to allow Him to soften my heart. Sometimes it was so hard as I dealt with pain from my past. Rejection and self-esteem issues were at the top of the list. I had to forgive people, especially men who had hurt me. And I had to allow Jesus to have a greater part of my life. He was a "man" whom I had to trust first with my heart.

As the Lord was working on the interior (as the original interior decorator), Mike had to deal with the exterior. I'm not sure which was more difficult. Sometimes the pain the Lord was dealing with inside of me was manifesting itself in my relationship with my husband, who was dealing with his own problems.

Mike's father died when he was little. Even before his dad died, he didn't experience a good model of marriage. I had been married before and wasn't very trusting. My insecurities were enough to sabotage the most patient, loving saint. And that describes Mike.

He told me once, "Gael, you can do everything you want to try and push me away, but I am committed to this relationship." Perhaps I was testing him to see if he would leave me too.

But difficult times were ahead for both of us, and sometimes the only reason I stayed in the marriage was my commitment to my vows to God. I knew God hated divorce (Matt. 19:8) because of what it does to people and families, and the pain it inflicts. I had already experienced that firsthand. So I had to allow the Lord to empty me of my feelings for my husband and fill me with His love. I had to see Mike through His eyes.

One day the Lord gave me a vision of Mike. I saw a picture of a little boy who looked like a Romanian orphan. I knew what the vision meant; Mike had been neglected, unloved, and unwanted. It tore at my heart. This was a man who needed to be loved and desired, but here I was an ice princess with a cold, frozen heart.

So the Lord started to knit our hearts together. He knew both of us loved Him, but our love for each other was not His love. Our marriage did not represent His love. We were not the poster children for a godly marriage.

Mike and I first met at church. He was a visitor at the church I was attending when the Lord pointed me out to him and said, "There's your wife." Mike had to ask someone for my name, as the Lord did not allow him to meet me until it was time. Eventually it was time, and he pursued me with a vengeance. The Lord showed me later that this pursuit was not unlike His quest for us.

Mike was wonderful during this time, but I was scared. We remained chaste during our dating because this time I wanted to do everything correctly. But I had a secret desire—I wanted to be a virgin again on my wedding night. No one but the Lord knew this. Then on my wedding day, before I walked down the aisle, a prophetic friend came up to me with a word from the Lord. He said, "The Lord says you are a virgin again." Whew, try walking down the aisle after a word like that!

As soon as we were married, all my fears were gone. It was as if I had jumped off a cliff into the arms of love. I went for it. But as instantaneous as that was for me, something else was going on inside of Mike.

The moment we said our vows, Mike changed. It was like Dr. Jekyll and Mr. Hyde. Something came over him. I hoped and prayed that no one would ask me how the first week of my marriage was going. My birthday was only nine days after our wedding and he forgot it. Where was the wonderful man who had pursued me with such passion? Had I been deceived?

Within months, we were in trouble. Leaders from our church came over and prayed for us. One of the team members got a word that Mike had made a vow about marriage when he was little. He had made a vow and a judgment that his wife would never be like his mother. Mike acknowledged that it was true, and he repented. Our relationship started to change, but not quickly enough for me.

In my heart, I believed I had been set up by God and by Mike. I was angry, disillusioned, and hurt. I thought that as a Christian I would have a Cinderella marriage. I figured marriage in Christ had to be different from marriage without Christ. But once again, I didn't know Christ's plan.

In my heart, divorce was not an option, although I did threaten it until the Lord told me to stop. Then He asked me the question on the stairs if I would do it for Him, and I submitted to Him. And once again, the Lord asked me to trust Him step by step and to follow His strategy for our lives.

One time Mike called me from work, and we had an argument. At the end of the conversation, Mike told me that he loved me. I said nothing and hung up. As soon as I did this, the Lord spoke to me, "Gael, you're withholding love."

"But Lord, I'm not going to just put a Band-Aid over the problem and say, 'I love you' and forget what he said."

"But Gael, what *you* did was wrong. You withheld love from your husband. The two of you are going around and around like gerbils on a wheel. Someone has to break the cycle. I am asking you."

"But Lord, you know what he did. Why don't You talk to him about it? Why me?"

"Because you and Mike are one, and you are the one who is listening."

I called Mike back and told him I loved him. And I meant it.

I have to acknowledge that things weren't bad all the time. Both of us were committed to each other and to the Lord. The problems went in cycles. We would do well for a time, and then our relationship would become explosive again. I never knew what would set off the explosions; it was usually something stupid, and we would overreact.

I would cry to the Lord at these times and He would help me. For almost three years, He told me not to say anything back to Mike when I was hurt, but to bring my pain directly to Him.

Once I was passing out blueberry pie to Mike and the kids. I was angry with Mike and just slopped a piece of pie on his plate. It didn't look pretty at all, and I didn't care. But the Lord did. "Gael, treat Mike like a king even when he doesn't deserve it."

Mike was unhappy in his job at the time and came home from work in a bad mood every night. The kids and I wouldn't even acknowledge him when he came in the door because of his demeanor. Then one day the Lord said, "Gael, I want you to smile at Mike when he walks in the door." I just gritted my teeth and did it. Over time, this gesture became easier and started to become natural. I think Mike started to look forward to coming home because of the greeting and acceptance he would receive. He knew our house would be a place of refuge from his job.

Another time the Lord spoke and said, "Name someone you would love to have as a guest in your house."

I thought about it for a while before speaking. "Lord, I'd like to have Billy Graham come here, but I would probably be too intimidated to be myself. So I choose Jimmy Bakker. I love what he has allowed You to do with his heart, and I think I could really be myself and talk to him."

"Good. So here is what I want you to do. When Mike comes in the door, I want you to get two pieces of masking tape with Jimmy's name on it, and put it on Mike's chest and back. You are not to pretend that Mike is Jimmy, but you are to treat him as you would treat Jimmy if he were in your house."

Well, I did that too. And after a week, my attitude started to change towards my husband. Mike, the good sport, was a willing participant in my reformation.

Another time the Lord told me to make a list of all the things I thought were wrong with Mike. *Oh, yes,* I thought, *finally, the Lord is going to listen to my complaint about that man He gave me.* But then He told me to make a list of all the good things about him. That list was over three times as long as the list of complaints. I saw the Lord's point and started to focus on the good character traits in Mike instead of the junk. It was amazing how the change in my attitude and treatment towards Mike changed his behavior.

The Lord also told me that the enemy had lied to Mike and told him that I didn't need him. The Lord told me to be vulnerable with Mike and not be afraid to cry in front of him. I very rarely ever cried with Mike because I was afraid he would think I was manipulating him. Now the Lord was telling me to cry and let Mike know my need for him.

One day the Lord said, "I want you and Mike to find a hobby together. Talk to him about it and see what comes up."

Well, this was exciting and good. So I went to Mike with a great suggestion. Why don't we go to garage sales and flea markets and find things and fix them up? Over the years, people had brought us things that we refinished, and now we were pretty good at it. We had made our own headboard, coffee table, Adirondack chairs, and I was remaking chandeliers. This could be fun.

Mike retorted, "Sounds like fun for you, but sounds like work for me."

I was disappointed at first, but then went back to the Lord. "Oh, well," I said, "He doesn't want to do what I want to do."

"What does he like to do?" the Lord asked.

I knew the answer right away. He loved playing his guitar. How selfish I had been; I'd been thinking about what I wanted. To surprise him, I got together with some girlfriends and started playing guitar with them. I picked it up immediately, and within two weeks, I could play simple worship songs.

Then Mike came home one day and caught me practicing. I told him it was a surprise, and that it could be a hobby we could share together. Within two more weeks, we were playing guitars together. It made us closer than ever.

A few years ago on our anniversary, the Lord whispered to me, "I knew you were the one who could love Mike." Those words blessed me. And then I knew I had finally found the man of my dreams. It took a long time and a lot of work, but we had made it.

Over time my heart was melting. I started to fall in love. This is from a woman who choked while even saying that phrase. I was not a romantic person, but I was starting to desire those times of candlelight and intimacy. The romantic nature that God has put in each one of us for His Son started to be uncovered. The longing between the two lovers symbolizing the love of the Bride and the Bridegroom in the Song of Solomon was growing in us. We had overcome through Christ's love.

CHAPTER FIFTEEN

Bigger and Better Homes and Gardens

The Lord teaches us about Himself in everything we do, everything we see, and everything we experience. Since He is our Father, He is particularly interested in what He desires us to know about Him and what He has for us through every relationship as members of His family. The Lord usually speaks these things to me through my own family, particularly through my six children.

All of my children are different. All six kids like different flavors of ice cream. They each prefer different styles of clothing. They certainly like different types of music. At any one time in our house, you might hear big band music, worship, and classic rock. As individuals, my children have certain likes and dislikes. But it is the family unit that binds them together; that is what we have in common.

I had a vision once in which I saw the heavenly Father inviting all of His kids to dinner. I saw an apron around His waist and a spoon in His hand, and He was excited because His kids were getting together. He knew that each one of them liked different foods, so He was preparing their favorite meals. But then Baptist called and asked if Presbyterian was coming. When he found out that she was, he said he wouldn't come. Then Charismatic called and asked if Episcopalian was coming. When Father said yes, Charismatic said she wouldn't be there either. Then Methodist called to see if Pentecostal was coming. When Father said yes, Methodist changed his mind too. Before long, no one was coming to the special dinner that Father had prepared for His children. In the vision, I saw Him sitting down at the banquet table—alone.

It was a sad picture. We are called to be a family with one Father, and yet we don't always get along. We don't appreciate our differences in tastes and styles of liturgy and worship. We are called to unity but not necessarily to uniformity. While we argue with each other and criticize each other, the Lord is preparing a feast for the banquet table and waiting for all of us to come together (John 17:23, Matt. 22:1-14). By looking at the individual family unit, we see a picture of God's heart for us and the individual love and care He has for each of His children.

One day I tried to hold my daughter, Allegra, but she was squirming in my arms. I wanted to talk to her, but she just wouldn't stop moving. She finally slid off my lap and left. Just as quickly, Max was in my arms. He was quiet and still. I held him tightly and spoke into his life, telling him how wonderful he was, how happy he made me, and what a joy he was. I wanted to do the same for Allegra, but she wiggled too much and couldn't sit still long enough to listen. The Lord showed me that He tries to do the same thing with me. He wants to hold me and speak life into me, but I am just too busy to hear what He has to say. It was an illustration I will never forget.

Another lesson took a lot longer to realize. Many years ago when the kids were little, they played sports. I love taking them to practices and watching their games. It's never a burden, just a deep, personal joy. Then one day the Lord told me not to sign them up for the next season. In fact, He said to keep them out of sports until further notice. I was stunned. He knew how I felt about team sports and the discipline of exercise, so I asked Him why He made that decision. He said, "You want Me to be glorified, so trust Me in this." I didn't say another word.

Some of my family was upset by this decision, but I had to hold firm. Meanwhile, the kids were getting older and developing their personalities. The child I was most concerned about was Peter. He looked down on himself and called himself names. One day he took a running test in physical education and came in second to last. He shared his humiliation with us. He was further convinced that he was not good at anything, and it broke my heart.

Then during summer vacation, Mike casually asked Peter to go running with him. He surprised us all by saying yes. It was not in his nature to attempt to do something that he couldn't do well the first time. But he ran. And he ran. And he ran. We sensed that finally it was time, and

God wanted us to encourage him to participate in sports again.

Peter entered high school that summer and joined the cross-country team. He was the only male freshman on the team, and he came in last in every race running against seniors twice his size. But he kept running. He won the Coach's Award at the end of the season. His coach encouraged him to cross train by joining the swimming team. He joined that and swam varsity, coming in last in all but one race, including the conference meet. He lettered and won an award for most improved swimmer.

Peter has changed. He has focus and goals. He has confidence. Losing doesn't matter; being on the team does. He is planning for the future. He doesn't call himself names anymore either. We are seeing God's hand on his life and see him learning lessons too.

Just as my heart was broken that Peter didn't believe anything good about himself, God showed me that it breaks His heart when we don't believe what He says about us either. He sees our potential and longs to encourage us. And He wants us to see ourselves as He sees us.

Then God did something miraculous and He intervened. Peter's turnaround has given me such hope. I love listening to his plans for the future. I love how he has gone from being negative and defeated to being positive and victorious. I love his attitude about losing. He said, "Mama, I'm here to learn everything I can, and then look out."

His attitude and humility have inspired me and caused me to quit striving so much in the things I do. That's a miracle in itself. But God wants us to be part of His team, His family. He wants us to run the race and not worry how we'll finish. He just wants us to finish. We're not losers; we're victors. We're overcomers.

By the time Peter graduated from high school, he had ten athletic letters in four different sports and was co-captain of the cross-country team his senior year. He was also a forerunner for his brothers and sister who have also joined the team. I can't help but wonder if my obedience years ago to pull my children out of sports enabled God to do a work in our family. And He is glorified.

Another area the Lord spoke to me about was discipline. Brook and Adam had both done something wrong and had to be corrected. I was going to restrict them when the Lord said that each needed to be disciplined differently. He gave me directions on what to do and I followed them. Both children learned more from their individual discipline experience, as did I. Discipline is more effective His way.

Alex is often hard to discipline. He is the most willful of all six children and requires care. He has a tendency to be more of a challenge. As I prayed about what to do, the Lord showed me always to keep in mind Alex's tender heart because not only is he the most willful, he is also the most sensitive. When he gets in trouble, it is often hard to remember how sweet he is. He is the one who wants to snuggle at night. He is the one who feels so deeply. Many of his actions are reactions to the pain he feels in his heart. But we have a tendency to address the outwardness of his action instead of the inwardness of his heart. Our incorrect discipline then causes more pain, and it compounds the problem.

Adam and Alex sometimes beg for discipline. When Adam was in high school he would set himself up to get restricted. He would get invited to parties in which he knew he would get into trouble if he went. He didn't have the strength to say no, so he would do something at home that he knew would get him restricted. He then had an excuse to tell his friends that he couldn't go out. It took us a while to see the pattern.

God has given us creative ways to teach the kids lessons too. Once we found some CDs in Adam's stereo that he was not allowed to have. We replaced them with Red Riding Hood in German, show tunes, and classical music. When he turned his music on and heard the German CD, he knew he had been caught. He sheepishly came out of his room and confessed what he had done. He also smiled at us and told us that we had gotten his attention. There was no big scene. No conflict.

Adam's friends were part of our extended family. One time the football team came over, put on some music, and shaved their heads in our dining room while we were gone. Of course, we found out what they were doing because they left their hair behind. I pulled out a chair and screamed because I thought there was a dead animal on it! Not only did they leave their hair, they left their music too. The rule was that if they wanted their music back, they had to ask me for it personally. Not one boy has ever asked.

When you have a big family, you need to have a sense of humor about life. And since we are made in the Father's image, He must have a sense of humor too. With all I have going on in my life, I just don't have the energy to get upset about every little thing. After telling Adam over and over to put his clothes away, I took his underwear and packed it into his book bag. The next morning when he opened the bag to get a pencil for class, tightly packed underwear popped out. During the next class, he opened up a book and underwear popped out again. He said he didn't open up the bag the rest of the day. Adam got the point. I couldn't do this with my other children, but with Adam it worked. It got his attention. He was corrected. And we all had a good laugh. As the Lord told me, "Love smiles."

It is important to God that we have joy in our homes. Zechariah 10:7-8 (NLT) says:

Those of Ephraim shall be like a mighty man, And their heart shall rejoice as if with wine. Yes, their children shall see it and be glad; Their heart shall rejoice in the Lord. I will whistle for them and gather them, For I will redeem them; And they shall increase as they once increased.

The Lord used this passage to show me that if joy resides in the hearts of the parents, the children will see it. Then when God calls them or "whistles" for them, they will respond and be redeemed.

It is important for the kids to see joy in Mike and me. I was pondering what to give Mike for Father's Day one year when the Lord told me to buy him a guitar. I was afraid that whatever I bought would not be what Mike wanted, yet I didn't want to disappoint him nor have my feelings hurt if he exchanged it.

So I confessed to the Lord what I was feeling. I said, "You are telling me to buy him a guitar, but I have a dilemma. Guitars are pretty personal, Lord. I don't know what kind of guitar to buy him that he will like. And I want this to be a surprise, but I don't want to give him an impersonal gift certificate. What should I do?"

The Lord gave me my instructions, and I couldn't wait to see Mike. He came home at lunch, and I asked him if he would like to go out. He was delighted that I would make such a suggestion. I even offered to drive which really surprised him. The kids got in the car knowing something was up.

As we buckled in, I asked Mike to humor me. I told him that I wanted to take him some place special. Then I asked him to remove his glasses and blindfolded him. Mike really is a good sport and went along with it. As we drove through town, he waved to people he couldn't even see. People stared at the van filled with kids and a blindfolded man. One woman looked at us fearfully when we stopped at a red light. She must have thought I was kidnapping Mike.

When we arrived at the music store, I told the kids to be quiet. I helped Mike out of the car and guided him up the steps and through the door. A saleswoman stared at us, and I motioned for her to be quiet. I then positioned Mike in front of the guitar display. Praise God! He had thought of everything. The guitars were on sale!

As I took the blindfold off Mike, I said "Happy Father's Day!" He looked at the guitars and then looked at me with tears in his eyes, smiling brightly. He was able to find a great guitar, which had been a desire of his heart. God's way was perfect! God loves to surprise us!

When my children were younger, I was concerned about spending enough time with each one of them. The Lord gave me a strategy for that too. He told me to keep one child up after the others had gone to bed. Each night we rotated, and a different child got to stay up for thirty extra minutes alone with us. It was a wonderful plan, and we were able to give each child our undivided attention to read, cuddle, talk, or just watch television.

One day the Lord told me that the Church would be judged for not equipping the saints. I was confused because I know many churches are equipping centers and train people well. But the Lord wasn't talking about that. He said, "The Church needs to equip the children now—while they are still children."

We can't ignore our kids. They need to be active participants in what God is doing now. And like David, we can't expect them to wear Saul's armor; it won't fit. If we tell our kids to be quiet and behave in church for the first sixteen years of their lives and then expect them to suddenly participate, they will end up being unprepared and untrained. They will only know how to be quiet and behave if they haven't walked away by then.

We have tried to raise our kids in such a way that our beliefs are not separate from our lives. Giving, sharing, helping, praying, and fasting should not be extraordinary things in the home; they should be the norm. It's a lifestyle. It isn't always easy, and we have made a lot of mistakes.

When I was teaching English, I used to do an exercise with my students. The first five minutes of every class was spent on a specific topic that I would choose. This exercise taught my students how to focus and to write quickly under pressure. I corrected every mistake that the students made, but I never gave them a grade for the exercise. My theory was that the students would learn from those mistakes, and many told me they did. I wanted to give them the freedom to make mistakes and then correct them gently without penalizing them. Now, if they made the mistake during a test . . . that was different. Consequences resulted during those times. During the learning phase, however, I offered a different level of grace.

God showed me that He is the same way. He knows when to correct without penalty and when to discipline with consequences. That is the mercy and grace of His love.

As a mother, I need His mercy and love when I make mistakes. I have done my best to take responsibility when I have been wrong. I go to the children and tell them I'm sorry and ask them to forgive me. I want to be a good role model. But sometimes I agonize over how I'm raising them and wonder if I'm doing enough the right way. I recognize that my heavenly Father is the perfect Father, yet Adam and Eve still chose to rebel. The Lord spoke to me through a friend who said, "If mothers were perfect, children wouldn't need God." As the Lord told me, "Holiness is not in being perfect; it is in being perfected."

But when it comes to my children, I try to listen very carefully to the Lord for direction. When Adam was little, the Lord told me to let him wear whatever clothes he wanted and wear his hair any way he wanted. If I did that, he wouldn't rebel. I followed His advice and it was true.

When he was in high school, we wrestled with his choice of music. Once again, I had to take his music away. But then the Lord spoke to me and told me to buy a CD for Adam. It was a secular band that he liked. The Lord told me to wrap the CD as a gift and write him a note:

"Adam, God is not a God who just takes things away; He is a God who gives." Adam was touched, and he learned something about his Father that day.

When Adam went away to college and got into difficult situations, the Lord said, "Let him know; then let him go." So many times I had to speak him, take my hands off a situation, and then trust God.

But another time the Lord told me I was a better mother before I was saved. He said that before I was saved, I disciplined out of a heart of love, but when I became a Christian, I disciplined out of fear. I was afraid my kids would not be obedient and would therefore grow up not obeying God. The Lord told me I was wrong. He said, "I want their love, Gael. They will be obedient if they love Me. That is how they will show their love. But your motivation has been fear—a fear of your children not being obedient to Me and of how people will judge you and your children if they don't obey." He showed me that a lot of Christian parents are making the same mistake. If we show love, our children will love.

And there is such blessing in that love. I knew a family in which some of the grown children had little contact with the rest of the family. During that time, only two of the siblings were in contact with their parents. The Lord showed me that the intimate relationship those children had with their parents mirrored their relationship with Him. And because of that relationship, the parents were in a position to bless those children. The siblings who were not in fellowship missed out on blessings that could have been theirs. It is the same for those who are not in relationship with our heavenly Father. Not only do they miss out on the enjoyment of having intimate fellowship with Him, but also they can't partake in the blessings that are theirs as joint heirs with Christ (Rom. 8:17).

First Peter 3:8 (TLB) sums up God's heart: "And now this word to all of you: You should be like one big happy family, full of sympathy toward each other, loving one another with tender hearts and humble minds. Don't repay evil for evil. Don't snap back at those who say unkind things about you. Instead, pray for God's help for them, for we are to be kind to others, and God will bless us for it."

CHAPTER SIXTEEN

An Eternal Perspective

Sometimes we get so caught up in day to day living that we forget the bigger picture, an eternal perspective. Life doesn't just end on this earth. For those of us who believe in Jesus as our Savior, it continues.

Recently, the Lord put it on our hearts to buy two of our sons new guitars for Christmas. He told us not to worry about the cost. He said that the plan He had for our children through worship and music would not only affect them but our children's children and many others too. That was a word for the future and much bigger than what we see at this minute.

Even as I pray for the unknown spouses-to-be of my children and other issues, I sense the future for our lives. I pray about all in my family who will follow after us. God spoke to Abraham and Moses about generations that would follow after them, and He is still speaking.

Through this I understand that my obedience here and now affects the lives of my children and their children. In Exodus 20:5-6 (AMP) God says He is "visiting the iniquity of the fathers upon the children to the third and fourth generation of those who hate Me, but showing mercy and steadfast love to a thousand generations of those who love me and keep My commandments."

God also requires that we not begrudge Him anything. Because Abraham heard and obeyed God and did not withhold even his only son, all the nations would be blessed and multiplied through his descendants (Gen. 22:16-18). My obedience affects my descendants.

Before Mike and I were married, we talked about having children. But then during our honeymoon, he decided that he liked things just the way they were—just the four of us. That was fine with me because Brook was thirteen and Adam was ten. I had thought that Mike, who had never been married, might like a child of his own. But I never gave another thought about having more children after our honeymoon conversation.

Two months after our wedding I was part of a ministry team going to a conference in Edmonton, Canada. One afternoon I was tired and went back to our hotel suite early. I asked my roommates to give me some privacy since I really felt the need to be alone in a quiet place.

I had just put my head on the pillow when I felt something brush my cheek. I bolted up instantly and exclaimed, "Jesus, an angel just touched me!" I don't know how I knew it was an angel, but I knew that one had touched me.

At that very moment, my roommate, who was supposed to be letting me rest, charged through the door. "Gael, I have to tell you something. I wasn't sure I should, but I just have to. There was an angel in this room last night."

"I know, I know. The angel just touched me!" I shouted.

My friend continued, "A bright light came into the room and woke me up. I saw an angel touch our other roommate and then it touched me. I asked the Lord what it meant, and He said we were going to have more children."

I was dumbfounded. I needed to be alone, so I got up and went into the bathroom to pray. "Lord, what does the angel's touch mean? Are my eyes going to be healed?" I asked hopefully. I didn't need or want more kids. What I did need was healing for my poor eyesight.

The Lord answered me clearly. "I promise you that someday your eyes will be healed. But you are going to have more children—a boy and a girl."

I have to tell you the truth; at that moment, my heart sank. I was not happy. I knew from Scripture that God has used angels to announce upcoming births. I didn't ponder like Mary. I didn't laugh like Sarah. I wanted to cry.

"Lord," I said, "Mike and I don't want any more children. I don't want to be fat again or sick anymore. You know how I get when I am pregnant. Besides, look how old I am. The clock is ticking, and it's almost out of time."

"Daughter," He said, "I want you to consider three things," the Lord said. "First of all, if I wanted women to stop having children in their thirties, they'd stop having their cycles in their thirties. Next, I want you to stop thinking about your age. Think of the eternal perspective. Your children will be with you for all of eternity. And finally, when you gave Me your life, you gave Me your body too."

Ouch! Chastened, I said, "Change my heart, oh Lord."

Within twenty-four hours, I couldn't wait to have a baby. Excitement breathed through me. I was going to have a baby. I was going to have babies. A little boy and a little girl. I couldn't wait. Then the Lord spoke again. "Don't tell Mike yet. I have to change his heart too."

I was obedient to the Lord. I didn't say anything to Mike. I started looking for signs of a change of heart or signs of pregnancy. Both came about the same time. One day Mike came home from work crying. "What's wrong?" I asked, concerned because he was so upset.

"I was just listening to the radio and the song 'Watercolor Ponies' by Wayne Watson was playing. God changed my heart about having a baby. I want a child!"

Within a matter of a few short weeks, we found out that I was pregnant.

I knew the first child was a boy, and that his name would be Peter. We decided to give him Mike's first name as his middle name. Peter Michael Hogan was born thirteen months after the visitation by the angel.

And nine months after Peter was born I found out I was pregnant again. I just knew this was our little girl. I asked the Lord what we should name our little girl. He said the meaning of her name meant "lively, sprightly." Again, knowing how much I love mysteries, He gave me clues.

I started looking for a name meaning lively and sprightly, and I found it: Allegra. It was a beautiful, melodic name. Longfellow even used the name in his poem "The Children's Hour." I was looking forward to the birth of our little girl. My friends had a shower for me, and I received beautiful pink and yellow dresses and bows for my baby. The excitement was mounting in preparation for the completion of our family.

Two weeks before my due date I had a dream. In the dream, I gave birth to a boy. I told Mike about it. We were puzzled. Then at what was to be my last doctor's visit, a woman approached me in the waiting room.

"Hi," she said, "The Lord sent me here to tell you that you are having a baby boy."

"No," I argued. "That can't be. I know what the Lord said after the angel touched me." But something in the woman's demeanor quickened in me. I believed her. But if I believed her, what did that say about my faith?

Later that evening I went into labor. Right before the baby was born, as Mike played worship music and read Psalm 91 over and over again to me, I looked at him, and said, "I don't know what is going on, but this baby is a boy." A few minutes later just after midnight, our new son arrived on Mike's birthday.

I looked at my new son. He was beautiful. He had blond hair. His features were perfect. In my mind I didn't understand what was happening, but whatever it was I knew this child was from God. And I also knew I was going to have another baby.

At 5:20 in the morning, I had what was to be the first visitation I have ever had with the Lord. I looked at Him and said, "Did I hear You wrong?"

"No," He replied, "But I had to hide this child from the enemy. You won't understand it now, but Gael, I knew I could trust you."

I knew what He meant. He knew I could withstand the very humiliation I was feeling at that moment. I had been open in telling people about my Edmonton experience after Peter was born. Since everything had come to pass as the Lord had said, it was easy to assume that this child was going to be a little girl. And while I was careful about sharing my experience, I wasn't shy either.

But now I was embarrassed. I would have to confess my mistake to everyone. I would have to contact people and return clothes. I didn't want to think about it. At the same time, I had to face the fact that I would need to go through a pregnancy one more time. I was disappointed about that too. Yet through all these emotions, I knew that this little boy was special. I loved him immediately. I felt protective. He had nothing to do with what was going on inside of me, and I was able to keep my emotions separate.

Later that morning Mike and I had to choose a name. We were totally unprepared for a boy, so we had no names in mind. Before Mike arrived, I asked the Lord what He wanted to name this child. The Lord said, "You have done all that I asked; you can choose whatever name you like."

Having a good name with a good meaning is important to me, so I started going through the Bible. But Mike liked the name Owen. I was mortified. No offense, but that name was in the same category along with names such as Orville and Wilbur.

I liked Alexander and Maximillian, strong, manly names. Mike said no. Actually, he said, "No way!" We were now at an impasse.

In all honesty and with full disclosure, I considered manipulating Mike. For a second I thought I might bring up the fact that I had just carried this child for nine months and had a very painful delivery; and I deserved to choose the name that I wanted.

Instead of getting into an argument or trying to get my way, I crawled out of bed and went into the bathroom to pray. "Lord," I said, "You know I could have manipulated until I got my own way, but I'm not going to do that. Please forgive me for even considering it, and I'm wrong. I'm going to turn this over to You. Your will be done. You pick the name."

At that very minute, Mike rapped gently on the bathroom door. "Honey," he said, "You can name the baby whatever you want."

With tremendous joy and relief, I called from the other side; "His name is Alexander Thomas."

Relieved not to have Owen Orville Wilbur Hogan for a son, I learned that Alexander meant "defender and helper of mankind." His middle name is also his father's middle name. Both boys share their names with their very proud father.

After moving to North Carolina, on the same night I sang show tunes a cappella at church (Chapter 13), and after sitting in a darkened room crying and complaining about making a fool of myself, the Lord had a surprise for me. "You're pregnant," He said.

I just happened to have an in-home pregnancy kit. Why I had one is beyond me, but I did. I took the test. I had heard from the Lord. I was pregnant!

I ran into the bedroom and woke up Mike. I dragged him out of bed and into the bathroom, and put the test in front of his bleary, sleepy eyes. "Happy early Father's Day," I cried.

Mike kissed me on the head, smiled, and said, "That's nice," and went back to bed.

I couldn't get to sleep because I was so excited. We were finally going to have our little girl that the Lord had told me about in Edmonton five years earlier.

The children were excited. Brook was now 19; Adam, 16; Peter, 4; and Alex, 3. Not too many people want to give birth over a twenty year span, but I knew this was God's will.

I noticed that I gained weight quickly with the baby and hoped that I was further along that I thought. I always envied those women who didn't know they were pregnant and just showed up at the hospital one day and delivered.

One day the Lord spoke to my heart and said, "You need to see a doctor." He led me to the one He wanted me to see, and I made an appointment. A few weeks later another doctor in the office, who said I might be farther along than I had thought, was examining me. "Thank you, Jesus," I quietly prayed. I was hoping I was about four or five months pregnant already.

But when the doctor went to hear the baby's heartbeat, she couldn't find it. "I want to do an ultrasound," she announced.

I knew the baby was alive because I had just felt her move the night before. "Lord," I prayed, "I know You're in control, and I trust You. I have such a peace about all of this. I know my baby is alive."

The doctor began the ultrasound. Nothing was said while we were in that darkened room. Finally, she finished. "I hope you're happy," she remarked. "It's twins."

My reaction was spontaneous and loud, "Thank you, Jesus!" I knew this was a double blessing from God. I just knew it, and I said so.

I couldn't wait to get alone and pray. As soon as I got in the car, I asked the Lord, "Why?" I wanted to know why He chose for me to have twins at my age and with four children already.

"Because you're a good mother," He replied. "And because you're courageous," He added.

Mike arrived home from work, and we went to our room to talk. He asked me how the doctor's appointment went. My eyes were shining as I told him about the visit.

"Honey, this pregnancy is going to be different," I started. "My age changes things a little."

"I know," Mike, the former medic, answered.

"But honey, there may be some complications this time that we have to be aware of," I said, building the intensity and mystery while turning around to the get the ultrasound pictures.

"Gael, listen," Mike intoned. "I can handle anything," He paused, saying, "Except for twins."

At this I whipped around, panic on my face, ultrasound in my hand.

"No!" Mike cried. "We aren't having twins, are we?"

My expression gave him the answer. Then I implored, "Mike, this is a gift from God. This is a double blessing."

The two of us went out to celebrate that night. But Mike just couldn't speak. He reminded me of John the Baptist's father, Zacharias (Luke 1:20). Happily, the muteness didn't last as long. Mike just didn't know how to deal with our pair of presents from the Lord.

I continued to bloom and grow throughout the pregnancy. It was the best pregnancy I'd ever had because there was just so much excitement surrounding it.

Finally, in the early hours of the day I was due, I woke up in pain. I quietly got out of bed and went into the bathroom where I leaned up against the door. The Lord said, "This is it. Here's what I want you do. You know how to body surf the ocean waves. Ride each contraction like you would a wave in the ocean." And that is exactly what I did.

Mike got up and took me to the hospital. My girlfriend was going to meet us there. Brook started calling people to pray. I had such a supernatural peace. I knew that in a few hours we would have our babies.

My doctor was just getting ready to go off duty when I arrived. God knew I wanted him to deliver the twins and not someone else from his office. And he wanted to be there too. With little effort, Allegra Olivia-Rose was born almost three hours after the first contraction. I had never had such a short labor or easy birth. And everything was going well when another doctor came in to assist and routinely checked the ultrasound. At the same time, my doctor checked the baby's position and noticed that something was wrong. "Call down to the operating room and tell them to prepare. We have a prolapsed chord. The baby's chord is wrapped around his neck."

Immediately people started moving. I was wheeled down the hallway to an elevator and happened to look over and see our friends praying in the waiting room. In the elevator, I saw the concern on the faces of everyone surrounding me. Mike looked scared, but I had such peace. I think I was even smiling.

I found out later that the operating room was ready because they were expecting another patient. Instead, they received me. I was anesthetized and fell asleep.

Sometime later, someone gently awakened me. "Mrs. Hogan, wake up. Your husband needs you."

"Baaaaby?" I croaked with a hoarse throat.

"Your baby is fine, Mrs. Hogan. But your husband needs to talk to you. He needs to know that you're okay."

"What kind of baby?" I persisted.

"You had a boy."

I know I smiled the sweetest smile. I had wanted another boy. I always knew one of the twins was my little girl, Allegra. But for the first time in having children, I had asked for a child by gender, and God had granted my request. He gave me another little boy.

"How much?" I whispered.

"Let's see. Your little girl weighs seven pounds and twelve ounces. And your little boy weighs nine pounds and four ounces. That's a total of seventeen pounds!"

My eyes flew open at this bit of news. I was surprised to say the least. I'm only five feet tall, and I'd just given birth to seventeen pounds of baby—one naturally and one by emergency C-section.

While we were in the hospital, we were blessed. Strangers who had heard about the twins brought us gifts. I was able to witness and minister while I was in the hospital. The night we came home, our cell group came to my room and we had communion together. After everyone went back downstairs, Mike stayed behind and washed my feet in an act of deep love and humility.

Members of various churches took turns bringing us food. People spent the night with the twins so that we could get some sleep. And blessings continued.

We went to church several weeks later. A new family was there, and I introduced myself. The stranger didn't look like other people who went to our church, but I liked the way she smiled. She asked if she could hold a baby, and I gave Allegra to her.

A few days later, the woman called me. She told me she needed help in finding groceries for her family. She said she called me because I had introduced myself to her at church, and I was the only name she remembered. I told her to come over that night, and I would have food for her. Then she hit me with a bombshell.

"Thank you for the groceries, but that was only part of the reason for calling you. The Lord told me to call you because my husband and I are to give you a car. He said you would need one with all of your children. You can't even go to church together right now, so we're going to give you one that seats six."

Mike and I were stunned. Strangers were giving us a car. All I had done was say hello, give my name, and hand over my infant. And then God spoke to them.

Not only did they give us a car, they became dear friends. Over the next several years, they would also give us a truck, and we gave them back the car. God blessed them with about ten more vehicles before I lost count. And we have not paid for a vehicle since. As with Abraham, a multiplication of life and possessions has come to us with our obedience.

The eternal perspective begins with life on earth, but it doesn't end there. Life on earth passes to a better place for those who are believers. And although I believed in life everlasting with my heavenly Father, I was also afraid of it. I was afraid of death. In particular, I was afraid of losing my loved ones here on earth.

Many years ago, a pastor told us that in some cultures, Jesus appears in dreams and visions, preparing families for the death of loved ones. That story intrigued me, and so I asked the Lord to do that for me.

And He did.

A couple of years ago, I woke up one morning to have a vision of my father in a casket. I was disturbed and started to cry. I tried to explain away the vision with other interpretations, but I couldn't. After talking to Mike, I met with a friend and shared my concern. But even though my mind didn't want to accept it, in my heart I knew what the vision meant.

The Lord put it on my heart to call my parents and ask them to go on vacation with us. I even knew where we were to meet—Hershey, Pennsylvania. It was a short trip for them, and the kids could go to the amusement park there. Mike agreed to my plan, and I called Mom and Dad. Mom responded enthusiastically. She said she had just told Dad that morning that she wanted to see us but was too tired to make the long trip to North Carolina. Meeting in Hershey was a perfect solution. So we arranged our plans.

My heart was heavy but blessed. I knew God was giving us this opportunity to make one last memory together as a whole family. We started our trip with a van that would not last much longer, and I prayed that God would care for us as we traveled.

When we arrived at the motel where we'd spend the next few days together, Mom and Dad called me to their room to talk. They were so excited to see us. Then Mom pulled out a box. Inside were a necklace and a pair of earrings that Dad had given her years ago, and she wanted me to have them. Then Dad said, "This is for you too." He handed me a piece of paper. At first, I couldn't comprehend what I was reading, so I asked him to explain.

Mom jumped in, saying, "Your dad was watching television one day and saw a commercial for used vans. He got up and went out and bought you one." My response was spontaneous. I cried and cried and cried. I sobbed like the little girl I am. First of all, I needed another car, and only God alone knew how I prayed for one. I also knew this might be the last gift my father might ever give me. My emotions were so raw. I was flooded with love, joy, and sadness all at the same time.

We spent several days with my parents and then drove to their house to pick up the new van before going back to North Carolina. I made sure we took plenty of pictures with my father before we left. I called my uncle and asked him to come over too. I wanted pictures of him with my dad. I wanted to make sure that I had recorded all of our memories.

I cried almost all the way home. I couldn't stop. I had to commit my father's passing to God and trust Him. But then nothing happened. I figured I had misunderstood the vision. I settled down and prepared to go back home that fall for my thirtieth high school reunion. But while we were there, Mike's mother died unexpectedly hours after the final dinner, and we had to leave my parents' home. I sensed an urgency when I said good-bye to my dad. I took special note of the way he looked, the softness of his cheek, and the smell of his aftershave. I knew in my heart that I had understood God correctly. Dad was still here to see me through this passing first.

Two months later, he became sick. It started off with a bad cough and developed into pneumonia. He was eventually hospitalized. Meanwhile, God was dealing with him. Dad was saved, but he didn't have the relationship that he could have had. His illness brought him to a place where he experienced the reality of Christ.

After Dad was released from the hospital, he was told that he had cancer. On that same day, we learned that Mike was losing his job. The Lord told me to pray two things: for restoration in the family and for Dad to go to sleep. He never let me pray for healing.

I asked Him to let me know when I had to go home. I needed to consider Brook and Adam, who were now in California and Colorado, since they would need time to make arrangements. One Saturday, only a few days after we got the news that Dad had cancer, he was readmitted to the hospital. The Lord spoke to us. "Get ready to go," He said. I was sitting in my van at my girlfriend's house at the time, dropping off one of the boys to play. I asked Mike to take me to Wal-Mart. I had to buy the kids proper clothes and get a few things.

That night I called Brook and Adam and told them to come home right away. Then I called my girlfriend to tell her I wouldn't be in church the next day. As we were talking, I had a vision—an open vision of heaven. I had never had one before. I saw people assembling from all directions to one place. I stopped and asked the Lord what they were doing. He said, "They are gathering to meet your father."

The next day I started to have doubts about what was happening. Everything I was seeing and hearing was supernatural. Maybe I was just being emotional. I called the hospital and was told that my father was doing fine. The prognosis was good. They said there was no indication that he was going to die.

This confused me further. Maybe I had fabricated this fateful scenario. Maybe I was exaggerating. Then the phone rang. My friend, who is a nurse, called and asked, "What's going on with you? You're really on my heart. What's happened?" I told her everything including my doubts. She said, "Stick to your plans and go home."

That night I picked up the older kids at the airport. The next day Brook, Adam, Alex, and I left for home. It was a relaxed trip because we were together and because the nurse at the hospital had told me that Dad was fine. I figured at the very least that we would have a nice visit with my father.

We were only miles from home when I told Adam, who was driving, to go straight to the hospital. The kids wanted to go to the house, but I insisted. I remember asking for my dad's room at the information desk and looking at my watch. I noted the time.

We took the elevator upstairs and walked past the waiting room. My brother was in there with a family friend. His face was gray. "What's going on?" I asked.

"Dad's dying right now, and he's waiting for you. He knew you were coming."

I walked into my dad's room to see my family surrounding him. His eyes opened when he heard my voice. He knew I was there. I hugged my mom and went to my dad's side. God gave me a word for him, and then I stepped aside for my children. Then Mom went to him. "Go to sleep," she said. And he died—less than ten minutes after we arrived.

My brother, who had been out of our lives for many years, came and hugged us. He had been holding Dad's hand at the end. God's two prayers for my family had been manifested: restoration and sleep.

As everyone cried, I rejoiced. I stood next to my dad, but I knew he wasn't there. The most euphoric feeling of love and joy came over me. I couldn't even imagine what was happening in heaven at that moment. I had seen all the people gathering to meet him in heaven. It was so awesome.

The next morning, I woke up for the first time in my life without my dad. But I was not alone. "Daddy," I smiled, "How is my earthly dad doing?"

"He's grrreat! And boy is he glad he's here," my heavenly Father said.

The Lord told me to speak at my Dad's memorial. I wasn't sure I wanted to, but since the Lord had asked me, I said I would.

As I stood to speak, two thoughts came to me. First of all, I couldn't remember a time when I walked into a room when my father didn't smile at me. And the second thought was that no matter what he was doing or watching on television, he always stopped to find out what we needed or wanted. He never ever asked us to wait until a commercial or until he was finished. He always stopped what he was doing for us.

That was the legacy and the inheritance my earthly father gave to me. What a picture of my heavenly Father! I have always known that my Father is pleased with me, that I am the apple of His eye, and that I have immediate access to Him. My dad prepared me for my Daddy. And I thank God!

After I returned to North Carolina, the Lord spoke to me again. It was time to grieve. He told me that I had to grieve completely. As euphoric as my initial joy was at my dad's passing, I now had to experience the depths of grief. I thought I would never smile or laugh again. It went on for almost two months.

Then one day I was playing on the worship team during a Sunday morning service. As soon as I stood to play, I realized I had returned to the team too soon. I had no business being up there while I was grieving. As I stood playing and lamenting, the Lord spoke, "Honey, there is someone here next to me. And I am going to allow him to look down on you because he has never heard you play."

At that, I raised my eyes to heaven and played for my Father and for my father.

CHAPTER SEVENTEEN

Never, Ever Give Up

And let us not be weary in well doing: for in due season we shall reap, if we faint not (Galatians 6:9).

No one will argue that we are a fast food, microwaveable, television remote, and cell phone society. We want everything to be fast and convenient. We want it now. Well, God doesn't always respond to our demands for immediacy. Although we may kick and scream and throw temper tantrums, God will always do what is best for us. Sometimes waiting is what's best. Sometimes persistence is what's best. Sometimes persevering is what's best.

In Scripture, Mary and Martha contacted Jesus and told Him that their brother, Lazarus, whom He loved, was ill. Jesus stayed where He was for two additional days, during which time Lazarus died. The sisters told Jesus that if He had been there, their brother wouldn't have died. They thought that Jesus had tarried too long. But Jesus said before his friend even died that the sickness is not going to end in death, "but it is to honor God and promote His glory, so that the Son of God may be glorified" (John 11:1-44).

When circumstances don't go our way, we have a tendency to blame God; we don't see the greater purpose when He chooses to wait with His answers. Sometimes He is working out a greater plan for His glory—teaching us lessons, testing our character, or testing our obedience. Whatever the reason, God is in control; and if we don't interfere, He will be glorified.

The concept of perseverance is sometimes difficult for us to grasp because it involves discipline, dying to self, waiting, and trusting. Matthew 24:13 (TLB) says, "But those enduring to the end shall be saved." Ephesians 6:18 (AMP) says, "Pray at all times (on every occasion, in every season) in the Spirit, with all [manner of] prayer and entreaty. To that end keep alert and watch with strong purpose and perseverance, interceding in behalf of all the saints (God's consecrated people)."

In other passages, we are exhorted to never give up in doing right (2 Thess. 3:13) and to be steadfast (2 Peter 3:17) because we will be tested. We are encouraged to be faithful, even unto death, and to hold on until Christ comes (Rev. 2:10, 25). And like Isaiah, we are to set our face like flint (Isa. 50:7). Perseverance is important to God because it reflects God.

Through these times of persevering, God proves Himself faithful and real; and He gives us further revelation of His character. These times are difficult and push us to our limits of endurance. Not only do we find out more about our Father, but like good athletes, we find out what we are made of too.

According to *The American Heritage Dictionary*, the word perseverance means, "Steady persistence in adhering to a course of action, a belief, or a purpose; steadfastness." Some synonyms for the word include continuance, permanence, firmness, stability, constancy, steadiness, plodding, pluck, stamina, backbone, bulldog, courage, and determination. I would have added "pit bull" to the list.

I believe perseverance is another element of our Father's image that He is working in us, like our ability to love, give, and create. All of these characteristics identify us as being His and set us apart from the world when we exemplify these traits through Him and for Him. Then He is glorified.

But God's perseverance gives us security in His love because we know He will never leave us or forsake us (Heb. 13:5) or as *The Living Bible* says, "I will never, never fail you or forsake you." He won't leave us; He won't forsake us; and He will never, ever stop loving us.

Working this concept into our lives, however, is another matter because it goes against human reason and our contemporary mindset.

Several years ago, my daughter was moving into her own apartment with a friend in another city almost three hours away. She was the first to leave home. It was painful, but we knew it was time for our little chick to leave the nest. The Lord told me, "Under no circumstances are you to allow her to move back home during this time."

I didn't understand what He meant, and I didn't question Him either. I just accepted what He said as I often do. Brook moved away and everything looked fine until a couple of months later when she called home crying. "My roommate is moving back home. What am I going to do? I can't keep the apartment myself."

The Lord's words came back to me. "Don't let her move back."

As a mother whose child is in trouble, how do you say no? But that is exactly what I had to do. I had heard the Lord. When another mother found out what I had said, she was appalled. How could I reject my daughter like that? She doubted my love for my daughter. She offered to make a room available for her.

I couldn't tell her, "Well, you know, the Lord speaks to me, and He told me what to do." I had to be silent and accept it.

The situation grew worse. Brook became angry with me. I am sure she felt that I was abandoning her. But I had heard the Lord, and I had to be persistent in my resolve. It hurt to tell her no.

My cousins who had moved to the same city had an extra room, and Brook moved in with them. Eventually, she got another roommate from Sanford. It was during that time that she met the man she would later marry. If she had moved back home, she would have missed her divine appointment. Brook realizes now that if I had not persisted, she would have missed God in her life too. But was it hard at the time? Yes!

I have had to persevere with health issues too. Several years ago, I noticed that clumps of hair were coming out in my hairbrush. This was followed by short-term memory loss. I would get lost in town. I left food burning in the oven. I felt as if I was losing control over the simplest of tasks. I never felt well. Then one day as I was introducing myself to someone, I couldn't remember my married name. I was scared. Of course, all of this led to anxiety problems and panic attacks, which developed into breathing problems and other symptoms. One day I ended up in the emergency room.

The doctors couldn't find anything wrong. Test after test revealed nothing conclusive. I was becoming more and more upset. I was frustrated and scared. I was afraid of losing my mind and going bald. I was afraid something worse was wrong with me. I was afraid of the cost of seeing more doctors. I was afraid of dying and leaving Mike and all my children behind. Then one day after more of my hair had fallen out and I had become hysterical, I went to the Lord. I sat on the bathroom floor to talk to Him.

"Daddy, even though You may slay me, I will trust You (Job 13:15), and I will worship You, and I will love You. And if I perish, I perish (Esth. 4:16). Lord, I know that we just can't accept what is good from You and not the hard things that happen (Job 2:10). So whatever You want from me, here I am. I still love You."

In my heart, I knew I had totally submitted the situation to Him and accepted it. I knew the cost was that I could completely lose my memory and my hair. I knew it. And yet I accepted it because I trusted Him.

All of a sudden, the fear was gone. And the Lord spoke. "Child, I am going to heal you by your birthday. You are going to be okay. And one thing I ask is that when you wake up each morning, don't focus on how you feel; focus on Me." I did and He did; He healed me.

I don't know what was wrong with me during those awful months. I didn't get better right away, but I believed and I persisted. The doctors think that stress accumulated to such a point that it started to manifest physically in my life. It doesn't matter, though, because my God healed me.

Other things have caused me to persist in my walk with the Lord. For example, as I've shared before, finances have been difficult for us. Our gas bills have climbed as high as $700 or more a month during the winter months. This does not work into our budget, and we have to trust God to provide for us. This has been challenging because Mike and I are hardworking people, and we want to take care of our responsibilities ourselves. But sometimes God puts us in situations were we can't. Sometimes we're afraid people will not want to receive us because of the way we live and because of our neighborhood. Now I know that is a fear of man and pride, but sometimes it's difficult.

One time we received a phone call from a couple in Pennsylvania.

They had heard about us from someone who knew someone who knew us. They told us that God had told them to move to Napa Valley, California, and trust Him. They said how they had heard that God had asked us to do the same thing when we lived in Colorado. They wanted to know if they could meet us and stay with us on their trip across the country.

Mike and I prayed, and we agreed to have these strangers come visit. We have done similar things before, and it's just part of our big adventure with God. The Lord told us something different this time. He told us to treat these people like royalty and give them the very best while they were here. We always treat our guests well, but this time there was that added emphasis.

We didn't have much money, but we took what we had and I prepared nice meals. I took out my new dishes that I had received as an anniversary gift and were still in the box. We cleaned and prepared the house.

Finally they arrived, pulling up in their car and moving truck. We stayed up that night getting acquainted and eating. We enjoyed a pleasant evening. The next morning I got up early and the Lord spoke to me. He said, "I want you to go to the bank and take out $70 to give to this couple. You are to plant into their lives."

I called Mike and told him what the Lord said, and he agreed. I drove to the bank, made the withdrawal, went home, made breakfast, and greeted our guests. They never knew I was gone. Over breakfast, the husband said he wanted to give me something. I said, "Oh, well, I have something for you." I quickly retrieved my purse.

We exchanged gifts, but I never looked at mine, nor did he. A little while later, they left for the West Coast. After they were gone, I opened up their gift. They had given me $700! They'd also left a card for me, and inside was $40 from a friend of mine in Pennsylvania. The amount paid our entire gas bill, which was due that day! They gave me ten times what I gave them. That's God's increase and provision.

Mike and I could have interfered and tried to find the money ourselves, but we didn't. God promised to provide, and He did. Is it hard waiting on God? Yes! But He is never late.

Some of our other trials are more public and more difficult. The

Lord asked me years ago to fight pornography in our community. It was not a fight I cared to get involved in, but I couldn't deny what the Lord had called me to do. He brought me together with other people from other churches who had heard the same call. We started an organization and received some public attention. I was not only the co-founder, but also the spokesperson.

This wasn't the only time the Lord asked me to take a public stand on an issue. Years ago when I was working for a business newspaper, there was a fight against abortion. Mike was passionate about this battle, but I was afraid of being arrested as some others I knew had been. A group of people planned to picket an abortion clinic, and I thought I could cover it for my paper as a story about abortion as a business. I received permission from my editor and a press pass from the police. But the night before the picket, while Mike slept peacefully next to me, I tossed and turned. I called out to the Lord for help and He replied, "Gael, are you willing to go to jail for Me? Would you put aside your reputation and your name for Me?"

His question disturbed me. I was hiding behind a press pass. I was hiding behind man's protection. On one hand, I wanted to fight for what I believed; but on the other, I didn't want to go to jail for what I believed. And I knew what He was asking me to do—lay down the press pass for Him. Lay down the protection. Stand up for what I believed. Take a stand for life. Take a stand for Him, and not be ashamed of the gospel.

I want to make it clear that this is not about fighting abortion. It is, however, an example of how we are to be accountable to God Himself to do what He calls us to do as individuals. This entire situation was between the Lord and me. It was time for me to count the cost of being a believer.

I continued to struggle for some time. My flesh was warring against what I knew to be the truth. If Jesus was willing to lay down His life for me, was I willing to lay down my reputation to stop just one abortion so that a child could live?

I put down my press pass and went to two major cities the next day to picket in a cause I believed in—not as a reporter but as follower of Jesus Christ. I never did write the story for the paper. The real story was what God had done in my heart.

Now the Lord was asking me to take on pornography. I had a lot to learn, and this fight was going to be a long one. I had to get educated. I was cautioned about the dangers of going against a powerful industry. There were times during the battle when I felt that people were listening in on my phone conversations. But I continued to go back to the Bible. There was never a time when those called to battle ever lost when they followed the Lord's instructions to the letter. I intended to do that.

Some people wanted to go into the store that sold obscene materials and deliver the patrons from pornography. Others wanted to take pictures of people as they left. Still others wanted to picket with signs. The co-founder and I listened to each idea, but the answer was always the same: pray.

The Lord gave us strategies during this time, guiding our steps. We met with the District Attorney and learned the city had already taken some action. In all of our meetings, unity was the key. If any of us ever had a "red flag," we didn't go any further. We didn't realize it at the time, but in retrospect, we saw that the unity strengthened and protected us.

From a legal standpoint, there were certain things we couldn't say or do. We had to be very careful. While pregnant with the twins, I spoke at one of the largest gatherings to assemble at a city council meeting. So many people were in attendance that the fire chief had to send people out of the building because it violated the fire codes. Because of my public stance, I became a public target.

Just a few weeks before I was due with the twins, I was subpoenaed in a pornography case. The night before the motion, the Lord gave me a vision of being a ventriloquist's dummy on my Master's lap. I joked to the Lord that I wasn't sure how I felt about being the "dummy." But I knew what He meant. When I opened my mouth, He would speak. And He did.

At one point, I was asked how I prayed about pornography. As soon as the defense attorney asked the question, she knew it was a mistake. I looked at the lawyers and the defendants and told them how we prayed for them, and for the men involved in pornography, and for the women and children who are affected by it. This was said from my heart and with tears in my eyes. The passion that I had not felt when the Lord first spoke to me about fighting pornography was now in my heart. This was His heart, and this was His fight.

We won every case in which we were involved. And although the store was not closed, it was fined; and the people who worked there were affected. Even in victory, the Lord told us how to respond—not with cheers and gloating but with love and humility

We continued the fight. Word was sent to me through someone in a very high position that I needed to be careful. I knew this was a warning from the Lord, so the Lord gave me new ways to fight the battle through my obedience and my lifestyle. He showed me that we had gone as far as we could for now because the adult bookstores have a legal right in the natural and in the spiritual realm to remain open. The bookstores are open twenty-four hours a day, seven days a week. The churches aren't. There is nothing to combat the sin here twenty-four seven—yet.

Tenacity, patience, grit, singleness of purpose—again these are synonyms for perseverance. God strengthens us along our journey so that we will never quit. Hardships do strengthen us mentally, physically, and spiritually.

One day I was picking up the kids from school when a teacher told me that the Gideons couldn't pass out Bibles at the high school. Her words wouldn't leave me, and by the time I arrived home, I was feeling such pressure that I knew I had to pray. I asked the Lord what He wanted me to do.

The Lord said, "Honey, Mike and you have given money for Bibles in China. You have physically packed Bibles to be sent to Russia. But there are children in your own county who have never owned a Bible. I want you to get a Bible for every graduating senior in the high school."

I was so convicted that I couldn't say a word. There were no cries of "I'm inadequate" or "I can't do this." I knew what He said was true. I had been through enough battles to know that if He was telling me to do it, then He would provide a way.

I first called a national ministry that distributed Bibles. I wanted wisdom and counsel. I was told, "Leave it to the experts and to people with more maturity."

I was distraught. I was looking for encouragement and help and instead found condescension and negativity. I thought we were all in this battle together. I thought we were all called to the spread the gospel, not just a chosen few. Do I need to be a nationally recognized leader to do the work of the Lord? The answer is no. I only have to be willing. I remember when I was first saved and people would call me a "baby Christian." For a while that was fine, but after awhile I grew tired of it. I felt like no one ever took me seriously. Then one day the Lord said to me out of the clear blue, "Gael, I only had the disciples with me for three years." The baby tag never stuck again. Maturity is a matter of experience. In some areas I am mature, and in other areas I am still a baby.

When I called this particular ministry, I wanted counsel. I knew what God had told me to do, and I knew I had to do it—regardless of the opposition. If the leader had given me a better reason for not passing out Bibles, I would have prayerfully considered what he said. But how much expertise and how much maturity does it take to pass out a Bible?

I know this sounds dramatic, but it is the truth. I put my head against the refrigerator and banged my fists against the freezer. "God, you told me what to do. Give me a strategy so that I can complete your plan. Help me, Daddy." I sobbed and sobbed for the children in our county. I cried for that man in ministry. I cried for my own failure in not seeing the needs right in front of my face. And I repented.

Immediately, the Lord responded. He told me to buy Bibles and to pass them out at graduation. That sounded simple, but where was I going to get the money?

I went back to the teacher who first told me about the Gideons, and before I knew it, money started pouring in from various sources. A Bible publisher gave me a great rate for the project and even helped me choose a cover that would appeal to the graduates. They gave me a timetable to consider so that Bibles would arrive in time for graduation. I learned about the legal issues involved, and the Lord helped me there too. He said, "Wrap each Bible as a gift."

I was able to get wrapping paper at a discount. Then a local businessman offered his upholstery shop so we could wrap and pray over each Bible. Another woman bought tracts to insert in the Bibles. Then the Lord gave me one more direction. He told me to stamp the inside of each Bible with a congratulatory message from the family of my oldest son, Adam, who was graduating.

I went to the Lord and questioned this. I was concerned because the families of other graduates were helping with this project too. But the Lord insisted. I sent for the Bibles, and they were scheduled to arrive three weeks before graduation.

Days before the Bibles arrived, Adam was in a serious car accident. He was on his way to a gymnastic meet with his girlfriend and her mother who were both coaches. When we were informed of the accident, we had to drive five hours across the state without knowing their condition except that they were alive.

When we arrived at the hospital, the first detail I noticed was my son's big blue eyes. "Mama," he whispered. I leaned over and kissed my precious boy's dark head. I couldn't touch him. Half of his face was the color of charcoal, blistered and black. His arms and back were burnt too, with second and third degree burns.

Adam's girlfriend was driving the car that hit a guardrail, rolled, and its gas tank split open. Adam was in the back seat near the tank, and he caught on fire. Skin hanging from his arms, he slid out the back window while the women, who wore their seatbelts, were trapped upside down in the inferno. They all made it out alive in a fire that sealed the doors and windows shut and caused the cassette tapes to be burned into the asphalt. But the Bible in the car wasn't even singed. God had performed a miracle.

Adam wasn't able to return to school. He had been accepted into college and was a good student, so he was allowed to graduate with his class. Graduation was even more special because of the miracle of his life being spared, and his classmates and teachers knew it.

Waiting for his classmates after the graduation ceremony were over 300 Bibles, wrapped and prayed over with an inscription from Adam's family. God had thought of everything.

We passed out as many Bibles as we could before a complaint was made and the police apologetically became involved. Even though I knew the law and knew that what we were doing was legal, we prayed and the Lord said we had done enough. Over the next few weeks and months, Adam and his friends passed out more of the Bibles.

It was a painful and jubilant time as we cried in our son's pain and disfigurement, and rejoiced that he was alive and graduating. He did heal. He is missing a few freckles, and there are what we call "dirty spots" on his arms and back. But his body has no scars. I could have stopped the Bible project, but I didn't. We had to stay focused on God's ultimate plan to get the Bibles out to our children. We are admonished in Nehemiah 4:14 to fight for our brethren, our sons, our daughters, our wives, and our houses. The enemy may come against us, but we have to "fight the good fight of faith" and "lay hold of the eternal" (1 Tim. 6:12 AMP).

We are exhorted to pray without ceasing (1 Thess. 5:17 NKJV), and we can never quit. We must persist in doing what is right and what is good, even when it is not easy and doesn't appear to be to our advantage because we don't see the big picture. God does, though. That is why it is so important to be in relationship with Him, hear from Him, and get His perspective on life.

I needed God's perspective concerning Mike's mom who was a difficult woman. An alcoholic most of her life, she caused problems for Mike and in our marriage. I really had a problem with the way she treated my husband. It was easier for him to accept her behavior because he loved her, and he didn't know anything else.

One day the Lord convicted me about the condition of my heart towards her after another serious incident. I was ready to write her off and out of our lives. With her non-practicing Catholic roots, she was tough to witness to and to love. However, God is in the business of loving the unlovable. It is part of His character that He also wants to teach us. We are not only to persist, but we are also to love.

So the Lord spoke to me. He said, "Gael, she is your mother. And you are to love her as Ruth loved Naomi. And as your mother, you are to honor her" (Ex. 20:12).

So a mother-in-law counts as a mother too. Ouch!

I gave the Lord my heart in this issue. Once again, I asked Him to teach me and to help me, and He did. Little by little, He showed me things about my mother-in-law— quirks that made her enjoyable. He also gave me a strategy. He told me when to send her cards and pictures of the kids. I would write her personal letters telling her what was going on in our lives because Mike never thought to tell her the little things that women find important and fulfilling.

Over the years, she changed towards me and towards us as a couple. She blessed us several times and wanted to help us when we needed help. Mike was a faithful son, always praying for her salvation in his quiet time and telling her that he loved her when they talked. She would always say at the end of a conversation, "God bless you, Michael."

Eventually she became frail and sick. She finally quit drinking, and we rejoiced. But the time came when she needed help, and health care was provided for her. She was lonelier than she was sick, but we didn't want her alone anymore. During this time, the Lord told me to write out Psalm 23 for her so she could read it easily, and I did. I continued to send chatty letters and pictures to her too.

One day I received a phone call in the middle of the afternoon from the head nurse and owner of the health care service. She was concerned about Mom, who was an extremely difficult patient. Serious problems needed to be addressed. At first I wondered why she was telling me all of this. Mike handled his mother's care, not me. And why did she call at home in the middle of the afternoon? She knew Mike was at work. But all of a sudden, I recognized that a bigger issue was at work here. God was in this phone call. I paid attention.

Finally, after listening to the complaints about Mom, I shared my heart. I said, "I'm a Christian, and I know what my mom is like. But there is a bottom line here for me and that is her salvation, and I want to pray for you." I did before the nurse could say another word.

Then she turned the tables on me by saying, "I'm a Christian too. I lost sight of what I really needed to think about. Thank you." With that, she prayed the sweetest prayer of repentance and asked for God's help with Mom.

Several months later, we went to my parents' home in Pennsylvania to attend my high school reunion. On the last day of the reunion, we received a phone call informing us that Mike's Mom had become sick, and that she had been rushed to a hospital. She was in a coma. Mike and I prayed throughout the day. Mike had always asked the Lord, "Please don't take her until she is saved." In the past when she had been sick and near death, she would always bounce back.

We prayed and decided to go to the reunion. While I was in the bathroom getting ready, Mike knocked on the door. I opened it up, and he stood there sobbing.

I thought—oh, no, Mom is dead.

But his tears were tears of happiness. When the head nurse found out that his mom had been taken to the hospital, she drove the forty-five minute trip praying, "God, this may be my last chance to witness. Please give it to me."

When she arrived at the room still praying, my mother-in-law came out of the coma!

"Helena, are you awake?" the nurse asked.

"Yes," Mom said.

"Do you want to ask Jesus into your heart?" the nurse continued.

"Yes," Mom replied. She did, and she repented of her sins.

And then she went back into the coma. She died early the next morning without regaining consciousness.

Mike never gave up praying for his mother's salvation. I never gave up on what God could do. The nurse, driving and crying out to God, persisted until the end. And Mom, stubborn to the last, gave it all to God.

Mike and I left for New York as soon as we got the news. When we arrived at Mom's house, we saw that next to her sofa bed were pictures of all of us and a stack of my letters. God's love and His persistence paid off. He never gave up on pursuing her. His heart's desire is that none shall perish (1 Peter 3:9), and I want that to be in my heart too. First Corinthians 13:7 (NIV) says, "[Love] always protects, always trusts, always hopes, always perseveres." I can't bear to think about what would have happened if we had given up on Mom . . . but God didn't let us.

CHAPTER EIGHTEEN

Fractured and Pieced Together

Throughout this book, I have shared the personal details of my walk with the Lord. Although God has His plan, I also have a personal desire that I believe is from Him. I want people to want Him. I want people to desire to know Him and the joy of being with a Father who is extremely loving and kind—not just because of what He can do, but also because of who He is. I am just beginning to explore the many facets of my relationship with my Father, but before that can happen to a deeper degree, there has to be less of me and more of Him.

Of all the chapters in this book, writing about brokenness was the most important to me. As much as I am able, I want to convey the pain and the joy that comes from being in that position with Him. Some of the most precious and most intimate times with Him have been when I have been the most broken.

The Lord who made me knows how much I love studying the definitions of words. According to *The American Heritage College Dictionary*, the word brokenness comes from the state of being broken. The word broken means, "Forcibly broken into two or more pieces; fractured; sundered by divorce, separation, or desertion; having been violated: a broken promise; incomplete: a broken set of books; being in a state of disarray; disordered; intermittently stopping and starting; discontinuous; varying abruptly, as in pitch: broken sobs; spoken with gaps and errors: broken English; topographically rough; uneven; subdued totally; humbled; weakened and infirm; crushed by grief: a broken heart; financially ruined; bankrupt; not functioning; out of order.

I have experienced every definition of the word broken in one form or another, and I am sure you have too. Each aspect of all of those definitions has another word associated with it: pain.

Our society has a way of dealing with things that are broken—we throw them away. Broken is bad; it is useless. In some ways, that is how we deal with a society that is broken—we have no use for it. So we all spend our lives trying to be perfect and useful even when we are hurting and broken.

Jesus came to change all that. In Luke 4:18 (KJV) He says, "The Spirit of the Lord is upon me, because he hath anointed me to preach the gospel to the poor; he hath sent me to heal the brokenhearted, to preach deliverance to the captives, and recovering of sight to the blind, to set at liberty them that are bruised." In this passage, we learn that He has not only come to save us but to heal all that is broken in our lives. Sometimes we stop short in our idea of salvation. We think that by believing Jesus in our hearts (Rom. 10), that is the end of the story. However, it is only the beginning. He came not only to give us eternal life, but also to do a work here on earth. He has deliverance, freedom, joy, and life abundantly for all that believe.

I was a broken sinner when I came to Christ. In a twenty-four hour period I lost everything that was important to me except my children, and I only had myself and my bad choices to blame. The night before I was saved I wondered if the answer was in Eastern religions. I remember sitting in front of a fireplace with a drink in my hand, wondering how I would get out of the mess that was my life. I thought that surely my intelligence would rescue me.

However, I couldn't think myself out of my problems. I couldn't change my situation by analyzing it, and I needed help. My intelligence couldn't rescue me. Only Jesus could, and He did. So the first area of my brokenness was the one in which I became saved.

I was a wounded person when I came to the Lord on my bathroom floor that day, asking Him if He was real. I had experienced just about every definition of the word broken in twenty-four hours. My husband was divorcing me; promises were broken; my life was disordered; my speech and sobs were broken with incoherent pain; my heart was crushed with grief; I was wiped out financially, and I was weak, crushed, and humbled. I was broken in every sense of the word. But

God is a restorer. He loves to put pieces back together. He stitched clothes for Adam and Eve after their sin when He rescued, covered, and protected them. And now He wanted to do to the same for me—stitching me back together, piece by piece.

I tried to help Him. After all, for thirty-odd years of my life I had taken care of myself. And made a fine mess of it too, I might add, but I didn't know how to keep my hands off of things. I was like a wild stallion with a strong will that couldn't be ridden. I had to be tamed.

That is when I learned about His brokenness. It is not quite the same as the definition in the dictionary—even though it often had some of the same results, like broken sobs or a broken heart of repentance. But it was brokenness born out of love.

Psalm 51:17 (AMP) reads, "My sacrifice [the sacrifice acceptable] to God is a broken spirit; a broken and a contrite heart [broken down with sorrow for sin and humbly and thoroughly penitent], such O God, You will not despise."

David wrote that psalm after he sinned against God with Bathsheba. God brought him to a place of recognition of his sin and David was broken, contrite (crushed), and repentant. Again, in our society we think of brokenness as a bad thing. We try to keep ourselves from being broken so that we won't be discarded. We fight God because everything He does is to keep us broken and humble before Him. Not that we will be continually crushed and devastated (which is the result of being out of God's will and being in sin), but so that we will be safe, protected, and will find true peace and joy.

As a wounded person before God, my pride protected me. Walls and walls of protection were around my heart and mind. Rejection and fear kept me from freedom. Like that wild stallion, I could not be used unless I could be harnessed.

I shot out of the gate quickly when I was saved. God had blessed me with gifts that were raw and unrefined. In my mind, I just had to apply what I already knew with what I was learning and I would be fine. But that is not God's way. He is not going to share His glory with just anyone, especially me.

So the humbling began. The hardest lessons for me had to do with self-importance, attention, and submission. These were born out of pride, rejection issues, and abuse by authorities. I went through some serious times of conflict in my life because I didn't recognize my sin. After I did, though, God would encourage me to look at Him and not dwell on my failures. He told me to keep going. Meanwhile, I alienated people, responded in my heart in very ugly ways, and was superficially submissive.

I knew, of course, the correct way to behave, but in my heart, something dark was being exposed. Sometimes I was so familiar with it that I didn't even know it was there until the Lord showed me. He was always gentle and kind with me even when I questioned His methods. Later I would realize that He was saving me from a greater wound.

Once during a particularly painful time, He gave me a vision. I was walking out into a street when out of nowhere, a huge truck came barreling down the road. I was paralyzed and couldn't move. All of a sudden, the Lord came and pushed me out of the way of the truck. When He pushed me, I fell away from the oncoming path of the truck and received some scrapes and bruises. He told me that if He hadn't pushed me I would have been killed and said that the bruises and scrapes would heal quickly.

That vision gave me a picture of what God has to do with us sometimes. We may be in situations where we will be devastated if we stay where we are, and even though getting pushed out of the way may hurt, it won't hurt as badly.

So there have been times when I have been in the wrong position, and God moved me. It might be a physical move like getting a job, or it might be a spiritual move in my heart. But either way He moved me. He said, "When I change you child, it is by conviction; it is not by telling you that you are bad. It will come from your heart, not your mind." This is part of disciplining the wild stallion.

God has also disciplined me in the area of self-importance. When I was set up for a major position and was seeking God for an answer, He revealed what was really in my heart, and I came crashing down off my pedestal. I was angry and hurt. He knew I didn't seek the position on my own; it was brought to me. But God spoke to me and showed me what was really inside me. He told me that I could not think higher of myself than what was justified (2 Cor. 12:6). Then He told me that I was only superficially submissive in my church—and the leaders knew it. I was devastated because I didn't realize it. When God revealed it to me, I was hysterical and in pain for what I had done to the Lord, my church, and my leaders. I called them and repented immediately. I told them that God had told me in no uncertain terms that He had chosen them to lead, not me.

When I made amends with God and with my leaders, I felt God's hand on my face. He was so proud of me, for I had done what was right. The joy I felt at being under His wing and in His will can't be explained. At His feet, I felt as though I were in a high place. He told me months later that I was now a good follower. He said that before a person can be a good leader, they first must be a good follower. God showed me that through these situations in which my heart was being revealed, He was also revealing my good character to my leaders through my responses.

God would not allow me to receive attention or recognition. Time and time again, I would sit and watch situations in which I was involved garner attention, but my name was never mentioned. Others knew I had either led or initiated the projects, and the omission baffled me and hurt my pride.

The Lord told me that desiring recognition was a weakness in me, and that He was making sure that I received no affirmation, confirmation, or inspiration from man. This was so difficult for a goal-oriented person like me. Not to mention the fact that I strive in those areas because I am insecure and lack confidence. So a vicious circle was at work inside of me. I can remember one pastor in particular who very rarely spoke to me or encouraged me, though I needed it so desperately. And God said, "No, I am teaching you to believe what I say about you and to you."

I had to choose to believe God. Remember, I am only five feet tall, and when I was pregnant with the twins, I weighed almost 200 pounds. He made me look in the mirror and repeat out loud what He said about me. He told me I was beautiful and loved the way I looked. I was made in His image, and people could see Him in my eyes. Doing that exercise was part of my healing and believing what He said. I started to lose weight when I started to believe Him in this area.

When people paid me compliments in anything I did, I was not to accept the words from them personally but know that God was the One speaking to me and complimenting me. By doing this, I learned in part to avoid the praises of people.

A few years ago, I won third place in an art show. This was the first time I had ever won an award for any of my paintings. Since God had not allowed me to have any recognition or attention, this victory was special—not because I won, but because it was from God. I started to shake and spontaneously broke into tears. I knew God was sending me a sign that I was being healed. That meant so much more to me than winning. In fact, I knew I was healed because I didn't get puffed up. I cared more about what God thought than about the recognition.

In this time of healing and restoration, He told me not to compare myself to anyone either. He said that besides being a trap of the enemy, there was no one like me anyway, so why was I always comparing myself to others?

One morning as I awoke, God told me to pray and ask His guidance before I offer an opinion about a person or a situation. This is now part of my training. While I don't have this down perfectly, for the most part it does keep me from judging and being critical of others and myself. It is so much easier to seek Daddy and Scripture to find out what He thinks and then line up with that.

Once, on very short notice, I was asked to speak at a meeting and to share anything the Lord had put on my heart. I did it, but then I went on a little too long because I was caught off guard and uncomfortable. When I was finished, I sat back down in my seat and prayed, "Lord, did I do okay?"

"Yes, honey, you did fine," He replied.

"Oh, Lord, are You sure? I really said too much. I went on too long, You know."

"Gael, you were fine."

"Daddy, You know I hate the word fine. Are You sure I was okay?"

"Gael, now you're being prideful because you didn't believe what I said."

I learned the definition of pride that night, but I also learned His definition of humility. He told me that "being humble is knowing you are nothing without Christ, and everything with Him."

All of these difficult lessons kept me broken before Him. Other situations—my Dad's death, my son's accident, and our financial situation—kept me broken through my circumstances. He wanted me to be broken as a way of life. He wanted that wild stallion inside of me to submit to Him. He wanted to put the bit in my mouth and the saddle on my back so that He could use me more effectively.

I was speaking regularly in churches and at a few small conferences when I pulled myself out of circulation. I knew I was a good speaker, but I was concerned that people were seeing me, "the dynamic talker," and not Jesus, the Savior, in me. I told the Lord I wanted people to see Him. That is when He got serious with me. He asked me to obey and believe Him in areas that required more faith and trust. I had to be emptied of self.

Mike and I visited a little country church to hear a guest speaker. My spiritual life felt so dry at this time, and I needed a touch from God. We had gone through so much, and I was running on empty. Mike and I went forward for prayer. As the young man prayed for us, I heard the Lord say, "Give him your ring."

I knew immediately which ring He was meant. I whispered to Mike, and he motioned for the young man to come over to us. I told him what the Lord had told me to do. I slipped off the three-quarter carat diamond ring that I had bought many years ago and gave it to him. The man was shocked but then told us how his wife had lost her engagement ring in the ocean, and how he had wanted to give her a new one. He said he would have the diamond put in a new setting for their anniversary in a few weeks.

In my heart, giving that diamond away was more than just giving a blessing to that man. It was part of the humility, the dying to self, and the brokenness to which God was calling me. In a way, I didn't give the ring to the young man; I gave it to God.

I was speaking in a Hispanic church and asked the women if they had any prayer requests. Every blessed woman in that room asked for the salvation of a loved one. Again, I was humbled. In most meetings where I speak or teach, I don't encounter that response, especially from every person in the room. And knowing the poverty and daily hardship that these precious women face, my own lack of what is truly important was brought before me again. I was broken.

I also have to be careful about finding my identity in anything that is not of Him. Again, we cannot share the glory with God. I cannot have my identity in being a wife, an artist, an intercessor, or anything that keeps me from finding my identity in Him. Several times I have had to obey God and step down from leadership positions when I have crossed that line. I remember saying to the Lord, "But Daddy, I don't have a spiritual resume now."

He replied, "Good."

The Lord told me a long time ago that I would do mighty works for Him. I don't think about it or how it will occur. But if I'm honest, in terms of the way we in America think, I thought that maybe God was going to have me speak before large audiences or be on television. I don't seek these things nor do I try to make them happen, but I couldn't envision how God could use me mightily in any other way.

After my dad died, my mom learned she had the same cancer he had. I was preparing to speak at a church when she called to tell me she was having a particularly bad day. Then I received a call from my cousin saying that my precious uncle was hospitalized and in critical condition. Then I found out my other cousin, the daughter of another uncle from the same family, had died earlier that same day. I was in my room crying and seeking God. How could I speak when I was so broken? "I have nothing to give," I cried.

"Good, because when you are weak I am strong," said the Lord compassionately.

There was a knock at the front door and some friends arrived. I wouldn't leave my bedroom, so my girlfriend came in to comfort me.

"Gael, Pastor J. is here from India. He wants to see you, and he has come such a long way. Please come out and see him."

"Debbie, look at me. I'm a mess. I can hardly stand from all the crying. My face is swollen and red. Please, I just can't do it."

"Gael, please. Just come and see him. He knows what's going on, and he'll pray for you."

I knew my excuses were lame, but I was so broken. I couldn't be a hostess and offer hospitality. I had no energy, but I got up and went into the living room where the rest of the family gathered.

Pastor J. lit up when he saw me, and I was glad I had come out of my room. We all held hands and he prayed for me. "Dear Lord," he said in his thick accent. "I want to thank You for our sister. Because of her word of encouragement when I was last here, I have responded to Your call to plant 100 more Bible colleges in India and reach a million people for You. Comfort her in this time. Amen."

As my friend prayed, the Lord spoke to me, "That is what it means to do mighty things for me. Your one word of encouragement will be used to save millions."

I was broken again. What revelation that just one word of encouragement can save a life, cause a person to respond to God, and change a nation.

I once asked God why He was able to use a well-known pastor the way He did. He said, "Because I can." I want to be someone God will use because He can. I have submitted to Him, and I am letting Him put the bit in my mouth and the saddle on my back every day. I want to be a good "horse" that has been broken in by Him and for Him, so that He can use me any way He chooses. I want to go anywhere He pleases, and I want to go with Him.

Today as I was preparing to sit down and write this chapter, I opened up an email first. In it was a note of encouragement from one of my childhood friends who is also a believer. In it she shared her love for our eternal friendship and for me. As I read her words, I was broken once again by God's kindness and goodness, and God's love filled my heart.

CHAPTER NINETEEN

Love: the Hippies Got It Right but Did It Wrong

I'm going to share what is happening to me as I write this chapter. The past few days have been very stressful as I work to complete this book. During this time, I have learned that the cancer in my mother is spreading; my sister has broken up with her "significant other"; our financial situation is a challenge once again; and I am having some physical pain in my shoulder that keeps me awake at night. And last night, the wind actually blew my daughter's bedroom window into her room!

With a heavy heart, I sat down on the floor to read my Bible this morning, and then afterwards talked to the Lord. Here was our conversation:

"Hi, Daddy."

"Hi, Sweetheart." (He almost always uses terms of endearment with me when we talk like this.)

"I'm not doing too hot right now."

"What's wrong, honey?"

"The stress and pressure of everything is getting to me. All this stuff about Mom—it's just too much right now. And I am trying to finish this book for You, and I'm afraid it isn't flowing."

"First of all, you are not writing the book alone. I am with you. I will help you with the editing; and we'll do it together, so don't worry. I want you to calm down and just rest in Me. And quit comparing your writing to others; you are not like them. They have their messages; you have yours. And as for your mom, she is in My hands.

"Right now what I want you to do is to stop and think about My love. Write about the things that I've taught you. Let it flow out of your heart."

After His words to me, I got up off of the floor with a smile on my face and went to my computer. The peace and joy were back. He was in control. God's love changes things.

The first taste I ever had of God's love was through the peace that flooded me after I became saved. I had never experienced such a warm sensation before. I was also flooded with what I can only describe as a clean and fresh feeling, as if I had had an ultrasonic shower that cleaned me inside and out. Later the Lord gave me a vision of a parent washing a baby in a bathtub. Most parents love giving their babies baths—especially the first bath. As we wash our babies, we inspect every part of them. Their bodies are so shiny that we can almost see ourselves in their reflection. Well, that is the first kind of love that I experienced with God, and His goal is that His reflection will be seen in us.

When our son, Alex, was about ten months old, I saw another side of God's love. One night I had fed Alex his baby food and was serving Peter and Adam some pizza when I noticed that Alex had disappeared. We were sitting on the floor in the family room, so I knew he couldn't have gotten very far. Then I turned around and saw him lying on the floor between the couch and the love seat. Something about the stillness of his body that told me something was wrong.

When I picked him up, he wasn't breathing and was turning blue. I told Adam to take Peter and call for help. Meanwhile, I checked inside Alex's mouth but found nothing. Not knowing what do to, I started to do the Heimlich maneuver when I heard a voice inside of me shout, "NO!"

I obeyed the Holy Spirit but was terrified because Alex's eyes and tongue were protruding. I was standing with him across my arms and looking up towards heaven screaming, "Jesus, save my baby; he's dying! Help me!"

At that moment, a supernatural force pulled my arm and hand back and then pushed it forward into his throat. I felt something deep down in his esophagus and pulled it out. It was a soggy piece of pizza that had adhered to and blocked his breathing passage. Immediately he started to breathe. By the time the ambulance, rescue squad, and fire department arrived, Alex was fine. But without the Lord's divine intervention, he would have died.

But I wasn't fine. I went into shock. The after affects of what could have happened overwhelmed me. I cried out to God, "Please, Daddy, make some sense of this for me. Teach me something about what happened tonight. I don't want this to be for nothing."

And He replied, "Just as you fought for your son's life, that is how I fight for you."

What a picture of God's love! He is fighting for us. He is on our side. The strength that I felt alongside me in that room that night as someone unseen pulled back my arm was a strength that nothing can stand against. It was powerful. Determination and purpose were in that strength. That is the power of God's love.

I don't always show the love that God shows me. Sometimes we have had difficulty loving the people in our neighborhood. Even though we've seen some changes over the years, it hasn't been easy. We have heard the Lord tell us to hold our position and establish a beachhead, so we have obeyed. After being robbed, shot at, watched people vomit in the street and defecate in our yard, we became tired.

One night after our next-door neighbors fired semiautomatic weapons, Mike and I were angry. We felt our lives were at risk, and we were mad at God. We cried out to Him and He spoke the same thing to both of us: "Love your neighbor." Until that point, we thought we had, but God was asking for something deeper. He was asking us to love people who at times are unlovable, to a degree of intimacy and relationship that would reflect His love. In ministry, it is sometimes easy to give money or an hour's worth of time to feed the poor, which is necessary. But sometimes we love what we are doing more than we love the ones for whom we are doing it. Mike and I repented, and we agreed to love our neighbors.

The Lord brought us several strategies to accomplish this. Our first Halloween on McIver Street, the Lord spoke to me and asked, "Are you going to hide out again this year?" For years when we had lived in Colorado Springs, we had avoided any encounters on Halloween and had spent evenings hiding in a back room with the lights extinguished.

"Well, what do you want me to do, Lord? Do you want me to pass out tracts or something?

"No, child, I want you to read the chapter about Peter and Cornelius."

I found the passage in Acts 10 and immediately had a revelation. God told me that opening up my home to my neighbors was acceptable. He showed me that participating in Halloween with motives for Him was okay because we were going to take the day back for Him. "First of all, child, this is the day that I have made," He reminded me. "And furthermore, I don't want you to ostracize yourself from your neighbors. I want you to be part of the neighborhood. The kids only want candy. But here is what you can do—you can welcome everyone to your home, play worship music, pass out candy, and pray for the children with their parents' permission. This will give everyone a chance to get to know you."

We did it and it worked! And to this day, no one has ever said no to prayer on Halloween.

The Lord gave us other opportunities to meet and help our neighbors. I prepare plates of food for neighbors; Mike gives people rides; and we go and ask people if they have prayer needs. Over time, this has brought us relationships with people on our block, and people have been saved.

One man who lived on the streets came around often to ask us for food and help when he wasn't in jail. I was making him a peanut butter and jelly sandwich one day when I tore a hole in the bread. We didn't have much food for ourselves at the time, so I tried to patch the bread back together with the peanut butter. While I was trying to do this, I heard the Lord say, "Would you give that to Me?" I reached over and grabbed two new slices of bread to make a new sandwich. God deserves the best and so do His children. Everything we do is to be as if it is for the Lord.

Lately we have seen a change in the neighborhood as gangs and prostitutes have infiltrated. Our block was targeted as a gang territory, and this caused us more than just a little bit of concern. We took that fight to the Lord since we don't wrestle against flesh and blood (Eph. 6:12). Within weeks the designation was dropped, and the activity stopped too. Meanwhile, I was given a chance to meet some of the gang members and to talk to them. I was never afraid of them. When I talked to them, I kept in mind that the ones I encountered were ones God was sending me, and I was so full of love for them. When I looked into their faces, I saw the softness and gentleness of good boys with a destiny. Of course, I always check my discernment for any signs of caution and danger, but I have been fortunate that the ones I have met are ones I believe God is calling to Himself, and I told them so.

The prostitutes were a little more difficult to handle. Like the gangs who had designated our block, one prostitute had chosen our house as her personal drop-off and pickup point. We were not happy about it. And then we were put in the awkward position of having to explain prostitution to our young children.

Once again we prayed. I knew Mike could not be the one to minister to these women, yet they gravitated towards him, so I asked the Lord for help. I asked Him to help me see this situation through His eyes. I asked Him for His love for these women because I definitely did not love them. Furthermore, I wanted them to stay away from my husband.

I looked for opportunities to talk to the women and was drawn to one in particular. I asked the mailman about her, and he told me what he knew. Finally, I could pray for her by name.

Months passed and Mike told the one who was using our address that he would take pictures of her and her clients if she continued. She politely thanked Mike for the warning, and the traffic decreased.

On Christmas Eve, as on other holidays, we open our home to singles. One particular year was no different. One woman just wanted to stop by and pick up a plate of food because she had to work late. There was a knock at the door and Allegra ran to the door with the plate of food we had prepared. She opened the door smiling and called out, "Merry Christmas," shoving the plate of food in the hands of the woman.

But the woman was not the friend we were expecting. It was the prostitute—the one I was drawn to, the one I was praying for by name. I heard Mike go outside and wondered what was taking him so long, so I went to the door. And then I saw her—the answer to my prayers, my

Christmas surprise. I went outside, overwhelmed by what God was doing, and just threw my arms around her neck, hugging her and crying. She cried too and said it was the best hug she had ever had. I told her that I had been praying for her and wanted to meet her. She fell to her knees on my porch, raised her hands, and started praising God. We talked about going to church together and about her needs, which included a place to stay. That is why she had come to our house. I told her we didn't have any money, but we would try to help. My youngest son, Allegra's twin brother, Max, gave his Christmas money to us so that we could help this woman.

Another prostitute came and we helped her too. Mike, Adam, Allegra, and the women went to a shelter, and Mike paid the caretaker for a night's sleep with Max's money. The door was finally opened to minister to these precious women. I went upstairs, leaving my company alone to just cry to my Father. I was so happy He had sent them to us. I was so glad for the opportunity to show them His love. I was so glad He had changed my heart.

But He showed me something in return. He gave me a picture of the Prodigal Son and his father (Luke 15:11-24). I saw the father watching and waiting every day for the return of his son. He was wealthy enough that he could have sent someone out to look for the son and bring him back, but he didn't. He waited. He wanted the son to want to come home. When he did return, the father ran to meet him, embraced him, and gave him the ring and the coat; he also killed the fatted calf in his son's honor.

The Lord told me that's what happened when the woman came to our door. Before she could even speak, she was greeted with love and anticipation. Food was thrust into her hands; I threw my arms around her neck. She was welcomed just as she was—a prodigal who was loved, wanted, and anticipated.

Sometimes I have misunderstood God's love. One time in the middle of the night, I heard a woman screaming for help. In fact, she was screaming for God to send help. I jumped out of bed, threw on my white robe, and ran out the door in my bare feet. I ran up the middle of the street to the next block where a young woman had collapsed on the ground, bloodied from head to toe. She continued to scream for God to send help, and not knowing what else to do, I grabbed her, held her, and told her that He had sent help. I prayed for her as she cried in pain and told me how she had been beaten and thrown through a glass window.

Medical help arrived, and now I was covered in blood too. The paramedics informed me that the woman would be tested for AIDS, and I would be contacted if I needed to be tested too. I went back into the house and woke up Mike, who told me how unwise I had been. Then I prayed about the possibility of getting AIDS because I was afraid. I realized I had made some mistakes, but I wasn't done.

I became involved in the girl's life after she was released from the hospital, but it didn't go well. Finally, exasperated one day after a scene, I went to the Lord. He told me, "Sometimes your compassion is not My compassion; and your mercy is not My mercy." I had tried to love someone out of my own resources, and I was wrong. Being involved with that girl was not God's will.

I also learned about the goodness of God's love. I homeschooled Peter when he was in first grade. By the end of the year, he was required to read a list of ninety-six words out loud. The day of the test came, but when I asked him to start reading, he hesitated. Each word became a fight. But I knew he could do it; I knew he knew those words. I encouraged him through each word. I didn't help him; I just kept pushing him through ninety-six words. When he finally got to the end, he was thrilled. He did it! But I was frustrated and tired. That's when I heard, "That is what is means to be 'good.'"

I knew what He was talking about. I always hated it in church when we would say, "God is good . . ." Yuck. I hated that little response thing in that saccharine, singsong voice. "All the time, God is good." I would think, *Well these people haven't lived my life. It's been hard, and God hasn't been exactly good to me.*

Now God was telling me that by pushing Peter I was being good. I was being a good mother who loved her son. I was being a mother who wanted to show her son what was inside of himself to strengthen him and give him more confidence because I loved him. And that is what God does with me. He pushes me, not to hurt me, not to punish me, but so that I will recognize what is inside of myself—because He already knows.

I had misunderstood His love and His goodness. I repented—again. God's love is not just in those warm, fuzzy times when everything is going our way. His love is also in the tough times when He is teaching us, disciplining us, moving us, and encouraging us. We forget that love is not just in the romantic; it is in the suffering too. Love is at the cross.

Sometimes I just don't understand God's love. Several years ago, He spoke to Mike and me and told us to put everything that we valued in storage. Everything. He said that the way we could decide what was important was to think of a fire. If we cared about losing something in a fire, then put it in storage. And He said, "This is a Noah thing." Those were His exact words.

The first emotion that went through me was fear—fear of being in a fire. Next I felt fear that we had lost our ever loving minds. The third thing that went through me was fear—what if this was God, and we missed it?

We prayed. We waited. We sought counsel. We were pretty sure we were crazy. No one packs up their belongings and just puts them in storage for no reason. But we had wanted to move—for years—and maybe God was testing our obedience first before giving us a house beyond our expectations. Once again, we were trying to figure out God.

While we were at church one Sunday, Mike asked me to go home to get something he had forgotten. As I neared home, I heard a fire alarm from inside my house. Remembering what God had said about fire, but still sensing there was no fire, I ran to a nearby church and grabbed a friend off the front pew begging him to come help me. We arrived at the house within minutes and found the fire alarm. David couldn't shut it off. The noise wouldn't stop. I called out to God and asked Him what was happening. He replied, "You are fighting me on this. I told you to get your stuff out."

God was warning me. The godly fear on my face said it all, and David knew something bigger was going on that he didn't understand. I tried to explain, but I couldn't.

I went back to church and told Mike what happened. I didn't say anything else. It was important to me that he heard from God on the direction we were to take. The next day he came home at lunch and told me that we had to put everything but a few items in storage.

This was something we just couldn't afford to do, but we did it. Everything including the baby grand piano went into storage except mattresses, the washer and dryer, dining room set, microwave, a few seasonal clothes, old furniture, and the television. The house was virtually empty.

After several years, I asked God if I could replace my torn comforter with a nice one in storage. He said, "Yes, you have proven that you love Me more than you love your things." Meanwhile, He filled up our house with new belongings and furniture. And what He gave us was beautiful. Our other belongings are still in storage.

God's love tested us. His love also purified me by breaking my attachment to things. We obeyed God in a step of Noah-like faith in something we couldn't comprehend or understand. John 14:21 (AMP) says, "The person who has My commands and keeps them is the one who [really] loves Me; and whoever [really] loves me will be loved by My Father, and I [too] will love him and will show (reveal, manifest) Myself to him. [I will let Myself be clearly seen by him and make Myself real to him]."

If we love God, we will obey Him. What He asks of us doesn't always have to make sense. But if we do what He says, He'll manifest His presence in our lives. That is His promise. Just because we do what God says doesn't guarantee that we are going to get something in return. What He promises is His presence.

When Brook and Keith were getting married, we didn't have the money to give Brook the wedding she wanted. The only thing she has ever wanted was to be a wife and mother, and she wanted the wedding of her dreams. We wanted to give it to her but we couldn't. After she cried to me one evening, I went to God and cried out to Him. He told me "I am Brook's Father; I will give her away; and I will pay for the wedding."

A week later Brook received an unexpected check in the mail for $10,000! That is the love of a Father who cares about the desires of our hearts and will provide. That is a loving Father who wants to show Himself real to His children. That is the very real presence of God.

I was at a school recital in which Alex was on stage singing. Forty kids must have been on that stage, but I only had eyes for one—my son.

The Lord whispered to me, "That is how I look at you. I only have eyes for you."

God's eyes are on each one of us. I was at a funeral when the Lord pointed a man out to me. I saw him standing next to my dear friend who we wanted to comfort and support. After the funeral, I asked my friend who the man was next to him. He told me the man was his younger brother. With my friend's encouragement, I approached his brother and introduced myself. I gave him my condolences and then continued, "You're going to think I'm crazy, but the Lord told me to tell you something."

That got his attention, and he told me to continue.

"The Lord said to tell you that He has your name written on the palm of His hand."

The man began to cry. He said another woman had just come up to him and had spoken the same words. We talked for a few more minutes, and then I left.

Later that day I went to see my friend at work, and I told him what had happened at the funeral with his brother. Tears came to his eyes, and he told me the rest of the story.

Their father, who had been buried that morning, had been in prison for murder but had accepted Christ four months earlier. There had been a private viewing the night before just for the family. While standing around the coffin, the younger brother started to cry. "Daddy always promised me that he would tattoo my name on his arm," he wept. On their father's arms the rest of the names of the family were tattooed, but the youngest son's was missing.

With that, one of the family members went and got a permanent marker and with the family's permission, the youngest son wrote his name on his daddy's arm.

But now a day later, God was saying: "Son, your name is already written on the palm of My hand."

Isaiah 49:16 (AMP) confirms this picture: "Behold, I have indelibly imprinted (tattooed a picture of) you on the palm of each of My hands."

What a beautiful image of God's unfailing love. He saved a murderer. He reached out to the man's son who wasn't even living for Him. And He let him know that he didn't have to write on God's arm with a marker because it was already tattooed on His hand. God does what He does for us because He loves us. We don't have to do a thing. His loving eyes are on us.

One day I had just paid the bill at the doctor's office after a visit and walked back through the waiting room to leave. As I walked through the double doors, I saw an elderly woman sitting there in a wheelchair. When she saw me, she gasped and said, "I love you! I love you! I love you!"

My reply was immediate, "Well, I love you too!"

She continued to say, "I love you. I love you" over and over to me. I knelt before her as she continued to pour love into me, looked into her lovely eyes, and told her I loved her too. I didn't want to leave her, but I had to go home. As I stood to say good-bye, I leaned over and kissed her face, telling her again, "I love you too."

As I reluctantly walked away from this stranger, I heard her still saying, "I love you! I love you!" Tears filled my eyes as I spoke to the Lord, "If we would just stay still long enough, we would hear You say the same words over and over again to us. And we wouldn't want to leave Your presence either."

The next day, still curious about the woman, I called the doctor's office. I told the receptionist what had happened when I was leaving and asked if she could tell me anything about the woman in the wheelchair. "I can only tell you this," she said, "The woman had a stroke some time ago, and when she came out of it, she could only say three words: 'I love you.'"

Three words. Three little words that have so much meaning. That is what the Lord says to us, "I love you." If we will only listen. If we will only allow Him to be real in our lives. If we will only allow Him to love us completely, we will see and hear in all that He says and does—His perfect love.

CHAPTER TWENTY

Experiencing His Glory

Jesus said to her, Did I not tell you and promise you that if you would believe and rely on Me, you would see the glory of God? (John 11:40 AMP)

A dying world around us wants to believe in a real, living God. The world wants to know if He is everything that we have told them He is. Unfortunately, the world (and some in the Church) wants God on its own terms. It doesn't work that way. God's world, God's rules. The only way we are going to reveal God is by allowing Him to reveal His glory through us. And the only way we can do that is by having an intimate relationship with Him and permitting Him to do whatever is necessary.

The day after I was saved on my bathroom floor, I went to church with a student of mine. I had never heard of the church before, but it wasn't dead and boring. It was vibrant and alive. It was different.

The pastor prayed for me after the service. No one had ever prayed for me before. He put his hands on my head and the first words this stranger said to me were, "God is going to take your rebellion and turn it around for Him." He went on to pray for areas that were answers to my own prayers that morning. I knew God was real and was listening. This wild stallion had just been tied to the hitching post.

But when I went home that day, I was hit with the realization that I had left so many people behind in my life that *believed* in a God, but didn't *believe* Him. Here I was, less than twenty-four hours old in the Lord, and I knew many people who thought that they were going to heaven but weren't. According to Matthew 7:21-23, some people who have prophesied, driven out demons, and done many works in His name will not go to heaven because they haven't done the will of God. Jesus will say, "I never *knew* you" (my emphasis).

As I indicated in chapter three, people don't have to hear from God in the same manner that I do to have a personal relationship with Him. God reveals Himself to each individual in a way that can be heard and understood in that person's life. He just wants to be included and recognized in our lives. First Timothy 6:21 (TLB) says, "Some of these people have missed the most important thing in life—they don't know God." Knowing Him is life.

Years ago, I was watching a television special with Peter Jennings. He was interviewing church leaders across the country and asking some tough questions. I remember specifically the interview he had with John Wimber of the Vineyard. At one point, John held the Bible up to the news anchor and said something like "Peter, I've made up my mind that I'm going as far as this Book goes."

Yes! Yes! Yes! What he said was so profound because that is what is inside of me too. I want to go as far as the Bible goes. I want to believe everything it says. I want to do everything God created me to do. I want Him to be glorified. That is only going to happen, though, when we get serious about what God says.

When I was sick, losing my hair, and having problems with my memory, the doctors had me on strong medicine. People came to my house asking me to pray for them. I refused. I didn't think it was right for me to pray for people when I wasn't in my right mind.

Well, after I was healed I realized that not one of those people ever asked if they could pray for me. When I told them I couldn't pray, they just left the house. Those people really didn't care about me; they only cared about what "I" could do for them. The revelation of this hurt me deeply, and I went to the Lord. He said, "Gael, they do the same thing to Me. They only want Me for what I can do for them. They don't want Me."

Oh, how that saddened me. Here is this loving Father who wants to have relationship with His children, and here we just want what we can get out of Him. God is going to be glorified regardless of what we choose to do; but if we are willing, through His Son, we can be included in what He is doing. How awesome is that? He'll talk to us; He'll walk alongside of us; He'll guide us and direct our steps; He'll share everything with us including His mysteries. That is the heart of a loving God who has set before us a banquet table and prepared a feast—not just for eternity, but here on earth as well. As a loving Father, He wants to be involved in every area of our lives right now.

However, a very real enemy wants to keep this from happening. He whispers doubt into our minds. He makes us feel unworthy. He says we aren't valuable. He points to destruction and violence, poverty and pain, and says, "God doesn't care about you. He isn't real."

That's a lie.

My son-in-law, Keith, was driving along the California freeway with his son, Caleb, when he changed lanes as he approached his exit. In his rearview mirror, he saw a car speeding up behind him. As Keith made his exit, so did the car. The man was right behind him. Keith drove to his aunt's home nearby, wondering what was going on with this guy who was staying on his tail. Every turn Keith made, the man made too. Keith pulled into his aunt's driveway only to be surprised when the man also pulled in behind him. As both men got out of their cars, Keith was still questioning what was happening. The other man came up to Keith and started shouting at him, using expletive after expletive. The man's young daughter was in the car, and she heard her father yelling and cussing. Keith, an off-duty policeman, tried to calm the man down by speaking gently and respectfully. His aunt and cousins came out to support him. As they did, a police car pulled up with lights flashing. Keith was confused. The man finally announced who he was: an off-duty California Highway Police Officer (CHiP). He was charging Keith with reckless driving when he made the lane change on the freeway.

The policeman wrote Keith a ticket and told him he had to appear in court. Keith immediately called his wife, our daughter Brook, for support and prayer. He called his supervisors and told them what had happened. Then he called us for prayer and wisdom.

When Keith went to court, he met with the D.A. who told him the seriousness of the charges. He offered Keith a deal if he would plead to lesser charges. We told Keith that if he accepted a plea it would be the same as a confession of guilt, which would be a lie.

Keith went back to court again a month later and saw another D.A. who told him that the only way he could possibly win was to get a lawyer and go to trial. But if he lost, it would go on his record, and he could even lose his job. The police department that Keith worked for said they would get him a lawyer, and he prepared for trial.

Keith's case finally went to trial. When his case was called and Keith approached the judge, he heard: "Case dismissed for lack of evidence." Keith was stunned. In all the discussions, he was led to believe that he would be prosecuted.

The irony of the situation is this: the accuser now has a letter in his file referring to the charges he brought against Keith. It will stay there for three years.

This is a wonderful example of how the enemy works and how God responds. We are moving forward, but the enemy hounds us, follows us, chases us, and tails us. Then he falsely accuses us of things that bring confusion. The world's way of dealing with problems is to make a deal. Compromise, though, only leads to the draining of our resources. When we are brought before the Court of the Most High God, Judge of the Universe, with Jesus as our Advocate who works on our behalf for those who are joint heirs with Him, the ruling is: no evidence! Case dismissed! No conviction! And the one who falsely accuses is the one who ends up with the record. He is the one who is punished for eternity.

I know a pastor, Bill Maye, who put it this way: "'Faith, hope, and love abide' (1 Cor. 13:13), but 'the enemy comes to steal, kill, and destroy' (John 10:10). The enemy steals our faith in order to kill our hope to ultimately destroy our love, God's love." That is the plan of the enemy. Everything he does is to keep us from God's love.

God's great love is the reason that He is glorified. When we allow Him to be part of our lives through a personal relationship with Jesus Christ, who died on the cross for us, He is glorified. He gets the credit. We start seeing Him in all of creation. The enemy doesn't want that, so he keeps us bound in doubt and unbelief through our circumstances.

So we have to choose whom we are going to believe.

Do we believe the one who keeps us miserable and unhappy, and running the rat race all day, striving for one more thing that we know will only bring a temporary joy or relief? Or do we believe the One who brings life abundantly?

Ultimately, it is a choice.

Several years ago, my oldest son Adam and I went to California to visit Brook, Keith, and Caleb. It was a wonderful reunion. As a surprise, and with Keith's blessing, we whisked Brook and the baby away to the coast where we stayed at a cliffside resort overlooking the Pacific Ocean.

The next morning, I woke up bright and early and headed for the beach. As I made my way down the cliff, I noticed the beautiful beach below. But then I noticed something else—the beach was covered with sand dollars! I couldn't take a step without stepping on one. I have always wanted to find a sand dollar, and here were hundreds! I was as excited as a kid. Then a man on the beach turned to me and said, "Did you see the whale?"

I said, "What whale?" And right off shore was a whale waving its tail at me. I quickly filled my pockets and hands full of sand dollars and ran back to the room to tell the kids.

"Brook, Adam, you have to get up and go to the beach. It is covered with sand dollars, and there's a whale too!" I exclaimed.

My kids didn't want to hear about it. "Mom, we're tired and want to sleep," they both said. Even Caleb dozed.

It wasn't that early. It was almost ten a.m. by now, but those kids would not get out of bed. I decided to go back. This time I walked to a gazebo on the cliff overlooking the ocean. The gazebo was deserted except for the pelicans surrounding it. I sat on a bench and prayed, thanking God for His beauty and the beauty He had created. An Asian man joined me after a while. We started to talk, and he told me he was a scuba diver. He had lived at that beach for fifteen years and had dived all over the world. I asked him if he had seen the whale below. Without looking, he informed me there couldn't be a whale. I smiled politely and said, "Yes, there is."

He persisted, still not looking; "I have been to this spot over a thousand times. I have traveled all over the world. There are no whales here."

"Then what is that?" I asked and pointed to the water.

At that, he finally turned and looked below when, at that precise moment, the whale came out of the water, opened its mouth, and waved its tail. The man just stared with his mouth wide open. He looked back at me and said, "You are a lucky woman. You don't realize what has happened. You have just seen a miracle. There are no whales here."

I quietly left as the man continued to stare at the miracle.

I returned to the room more excited than before. "Kids, I just learned that the whale is a miracle! Whales don't come here! You have to get up and see this miracle!"

Adam put a pillow over his head. Brook mumbled something about washing her hair first.

I tried one more time. "Kids, please get up and at least look out the window."

This time they did get up, but when they looked out the window, they couldn't see anything. A fog had moved in so quickly that in the moment it took the kids to look out the window it was too late. The miracle was gone.

God doesn't want us to miss out on anything He is doing. We still have time to respond. We still have time to participate fully in His glorious plan. We don't want it said that we analyzed until we were paralyzed. And we just can't presume upon God's grace, mercy, or timing. We have to be watchful; we can't remain asleep. We have to wake up to what He is doing or we will miss out.

I missed out once. My dear friend Shirley had written me a letter about the current state of her life. She wasn't happy, and she had so many questions. She asked me about Jesus and what He meant to me. I was going through a challenging time when I received the letter and couldn't respond. How could I answer her questions when I didn't have answers for my own life? I put the letter off for days and then weeks. I thought, I'll just write when I have it all together. But something kept nagging at me, and I knew I had to write her back. Finally, one morning I decided to write her and tell her the truth. I didn't have the answers, but I knew who did. And I knew where to find the answers. Even though I wanted to be this perfect poster child for Christ, I wasn't. It's not about me anyway. It's about Him.

At last, I was comfortable with a reply and sat down at my desk to write my dear friend. But I never got to write that letter. At that very moment when I sat down, the phone rang. A friend called to tell me that Shirley was dead! I screamed into the phone, wailing in grief-stricken pain, collapsing to the floor. My friend on the phone couldn't quite comprehend the degree of my pain. He didn't know what I knew; I had missed it. I had missed an opportunity because of my pride.

I don't ever want to miss out on anything God is doing or has for me again. In Mark 16:15-18 (KJV), Jesus says, "Go ye into all the world, and preach the gospel to every creature. He that believeth and is baptized shall be saved; but he that believeth not shall be damned. And these signs shall follow them that believe; In my name shall they cast out devils; they shall speak with new tongues; they shall take up serpents; and if they drink any deadly thing, it shall not hurt them; they shall lay hands on the sick, and they shall recover."

I don't know about you, but I believe and not all of these signs are following me! I know I am nothing without Christ, but I still don't know who Christ is in me.

If we knew who Christ was in us, we would see more of the things that are promised in the Bible coming to pass. I believe that as we continue, we will see more and more manifestations of God's presence. We are starting to see some of these things in their infancy, but God wants more. The day is coming when manifestations of God's presence will no longer be considered supernatural, but natural—not uncommon, but common. I believe we will see more healings and miracles, and more signs and wonders. But God has to do a work in us first—and we have to choose to let Him. We must respond to Him.

Second Corinthians 3:18 (KJV) says, "But we all, with open face beholding as in a glass the glory of the Lord, are changed into the same image from glory to glory, even as by the Holy Spirit." If we respond to God and allow Him to change us into His image through each circumstance and each trial, His glory will be revealed. And that's just it—it will be His glory, not ours. His glory cannot be tainted with man's pride. We cannot assume ownership of anything He does.

As we enter into an intimate relationship with God, He will work all these things out in us, and then His kingdom will come on earth as it is in heaven. It is the King who will be in His glory and His splendor. The result of our intimacy with God is reflected in the glory of His presence, the manifestation of His purpose, and the kingdom of His plan.

We are running a great race, and we are not alone. God is cheering us on to victory. He is our Father, our coach, our timekeeper, and our personal cheerleader. He is overseeing every aspect of this race. He wants us to finish; and He wants us to win. Everyone who finishes the race wins. He is also the One who crowns us when we finish, and He is the victory.

One of my sons wanted to play baseball in the worst way. He had tried out one year and got cut, but he kept dreaming and practicing. He decided to try out again when tryouts came around the next year, but then he froze. He just couldn't do it. He was so afraid of failing again that he turned around and went back home. He found out the next day at school that the coaches decided not to cut anyone after all. And that year, the baseball team became state champions.

Don't be afraid to dream and let God fulfill your destiny. Don't be afraid to run the race. Don't let the fear of the unknown stop you from going forward. Don't let pride hold you back. God is able. He loves you so much. He'll show you the way; and He'll show you how. Just ask Him.

Perhaps you're asking, "Can God help me fulfill my destiny? Can God help me out of debt? Can He heal my illness? Will He give me the desires of my heart? Will He speak into my life? Would He do it for me?" And the answer is yes, yes, yes, yes, yes, and Yes! Acts 10:34 (AMP) says, "God shows no partiality and is no respecter of persons." He will; He can; and He wants to do it for you!

And He is asking you, dear one, "Would you let Me come into your life? Would you let Me help you? Would you let Me transform you? Would you let Me restore you? Would you let Me love you? Would you do it for Me?"

About the Author

Gael B. Hogan, who grew up near Valley Forge, PA, is known for her honest transparency, dry humor, and bubbly personality. Her desire is for people to know how truly real God is, and how He desires to be part of every aspect of our lives. With a gift for expression, she is a teacher, speaker, writer, and artist. But her biggest accomplishment is being a wife, mother of six, and grandmother of fourteen. She and her husband, Mike, are chaplains with International Fellowship of Chaplains, and live in Sanford, NC.

To contact Gael for speaking engagements or book interviews, email her at drgaelbhogan@yahoo.com.